31/5/96

Dear Sue

I do hope this book
inspires you to make
many beautiful
heirlooms!
Enjoy the kits.
Kind regards

Di van Niekerk

STEP·BY·STEP
CANDLEWICK
PROJECTS

STEP-BY-STEP

CANDLEWICK
PROJECTS

DI VAN NIEKERK

PHOTOGRAPHY BY CRAIG FRASER

AUTHOR'S ACKNOWLEDGEMENTS

Creating a book involves not only the author but also a supportive and dedicated team, and I'd like to thank my husband and friend, André, for all his patience; my two boys, Ryan and Brandon, for understanding when their mom was busy with 'The Book'; my mother, Joan, for her inspiration; Lisah Merementsi, without whom this book would never have happened – thank you for the long hours spent helping embroider the designs – and Joyce for keeping the home fires burning.

A special word of appreciation to Glynne Williamson of Struik Publishers for all her assistance, Odette Marais for her expertise and Linda de Villiers for her support. Credit must also be given to Craig Fraser for the wonderful photography, stylist Shelley Street for her patience and flair, and their assistants Bev de Jager and Vik Norval.

We are grateful, too, to the owners of the beautiful homes we used for photography: Rod and Helena MacPhail of Leeuwenvoet House, Yvonne Romano's Mediterranean Villa, Cookery School and Dining Club, and Dirk Odendaal from Riedehein House.

Last, but not least, thanks to White Cottage, Underberg, for their gorgeous linen.

Struik Publishers (Pty) Ltd
(a member of The Struik Publishing Group (Pty) Ltd)
Cornelis Struik House
80 McKenzie Street
Cape Town 8001

Reg. No.: 63/00203/07

First published in 1995

EDITOR   Glynne Williamson
DESIGNER   Odette Marais
COVER DESIGN   Odette Marais
PHOTOGRAPHER   Craig Fraser
STYLIST   Shelley Street
ILLUSTRATIONS   Steven Felmore
PATTERN ILLUSTRATIONS   Clarence Clarke

TYPESETTING   Struik DTP
REPRODUCTION   Hirt & Carter (Pty) Ltd, Cape Town
PRINTING AND BINDING   Tien Wah Press (Pte.) Ltd, Singapore

ISBN 1 86825 698 7

Supplies, additional patterns and kits are available from
Handicraft Designs, P O Box 447, Underberg 4590, Natal, South Africa.

PUBLISHER'S NOTE   Imperial measurements have been adjusted
or rounded up or down as appropriate to help the reader.

CONTENTS

INTRODUCTION

Candlewicking has been with us since the late eighteenth century, the basic stitches originating in England and the craft later spreading to the American Colonies. In the last decade, this lovely, simple form of embroidery has become popular again. Some of you will be familiar with candlewick embroidery, but I've written this book especially for beginners, with easy step-by-step instructions to enable you to create beautiful and original articles. Likewise, the more experienced needlewoman who has grown tired of traditional candlewicking will discover plenty of new, inspiring ideas here.

I've also explained the quilting technique which is often used in conjunction with candlewick embroidery. With quilting, most stitches are made by sewing through different layers of fabric, creating a soft, three-dimensional effect. Working through various layers of fabric prevents your work from puckering and pulling out of shape. Most of the stitches used to quilt these projects are made through all the layers of fabric, batting/wadding and muslin. This technique differs from the traditional form of candlewicking, but the quilted stitches are surprisingly easy to master.

There are so many beautiful fabrics and threads available today that I couldn't resist breaking away from the traditional approach to candlewicking of only using unbleached cotton or muslin. Experimenting with different textures and colours,

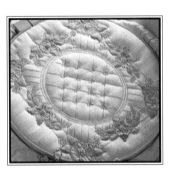

I found silky fabrics a perfect medium as they wash and wear extremely well and are easy to work with, plus they give a sophisticated, elegant look. Silky fabrics come in a beautiful range of colours and this gives you the freedom to be more creative. By studying the photographs in this book, you will soon realise how important colour is and how to use it to its full potential. I found that my students were very enthusiastic about the designs, threads and fabrics used to make up these projects and they were thrilled with the results – I have no doubt that you will be delighted with your finished projects too!

I've also used different textured coloured threads which are available at most haberdashery shops. This book will show you how to combine coloured embroidery threads, and even silk ribbon, to create a totally new candlewicking look. I will also show you how to use fabric shapes and candlewicking together – instead of having to fill a flower or a leaf with time-consuming embroidery stitches, a fabric shape can be cut out and the edges candlewicked with French or colonial knots. I encourage beginners to try this effective, easy-to-follow art form.

I hope that you enjoy this book and that you find candlewick embroidery as rewarding as I do – I'm certain that many of your creations will one day become treasured family heirlooms!

HOW DOES THIS BOOK WORK?

Each pattern is drawn to scale so no enlarging is necessary, and each design is named for easy reference. The patterns begin on page 65.

The first 17 designs are quarter or half designs. These are joined to form a pattern approximately 41 cm (16 in) square and are suitable for making cushions or quilt blocks. The quilt blocks are designed to form a set but are made separately and joined later. To avoid having to repeat a design more than once, a different pattern may be used for each quilt block. There are two designs for making framed pictures – these are also suitable for making cushions.

I have also included 11 other designs which can be used to make attractive gifts and soft furnishings for the home, each with its own set of instructions for easy reference.

All of these designs can be used for other crafts, such as appliqué, which I have explained briefly on page 33, *How to use these designs for machine appliqué*. You may also like to use the patterns for stencilling, shadow appliqué, painting on silk, ribbon work, trapunto or plain quilting. These versatile designs will be an asset to any pattern collector.

HOW DO I TRACE AND JOIN THE QUARTER PATTERNS?

Each pattern is drawn to scale so no enlarging is necessary.
1. Trace each quarter pattern onto an A4 sheet of tracing paper.

FIG. 1A ALASKA PATTERN – *one quarter*

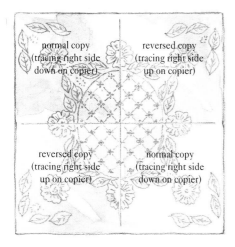

FIG. 1B JOIN WITH TAPE

2. Use a dark or black fineliner pen to do the tracing *(figs. 1a and 1b)*.

3. Trace the pattern as neatly and as accurately as possible. Use a ruler to draw straight lines. When tracing a circle, use a dotted (broken) line.

4. Make photocopies according to the instructions next to each design *(figs. 1c and 1d)*.

✦ In order to have four quarters which join neatly and accurately, copies of the tracing are made on the photocopier.

✦ When instructed to make a reversed copy, turn the tracing *right side up* on the photocopier.

✦ The black ink shows through the tracing when it is reversed.

✦ To make a normal copy, place the tracing *right side down* on the copier.

✦ Once you have photocopied the four quarters, carefully join with

FIG.1C CLIMBING TALISMAN – *two quarters*

FIG. 1D JOIN WITH TAPE

YOUR FIRST TASK IS TO TRACE AND JOIN THE QUARTER PATTERNS

transparent tape. Cut away the excess paper to make a square pattern.

❖ The patterns for the smaller projects are full size and therefore no joining will be necessary.

❖ To enlarge the pattern for a wall-hanging or continental pillow, for example, use the tracing as above and enlarge all copies on the photocopier. Reverse the tracing as instructed and join the enlarged quarters with tape.

HINTS

❖ *The neater the tracing from the book, the neater the finished article will be. Any lines drawn crooked will remain crooked on your finished block.*

❖ *Use good quality tracing paper which does not crease easily and is transparent.*

❖ *Name each pattern for easy reference.*

❖ *When joining circular shapes, rather concentrate on joining them to form a perfect circle. If flowers and leaves mismatch by a tiny amount, it will not be noticeable in the design.*

❖ *If you do not have access to a photocopier, trace the pattern from the book onto tracing paper. Reverse one or two as instructed and join.*

MATERIAL REQUIREMENTS

Which fabrics and colours should I choose?

Candlewicking was originally done on cotton cloth – when these fabrics were scarce, colonial women used alternatives such as old flour bags to embroider on. Fortunately, there is an enormous selection of fabrics available today. Why not make use of these attractive options to embroider a more sophisticated article which is elegant, yet practical?

I use polyester silk (polysilk) or polyester taffeta as my medium for many of the projects. Polysilk looks like silk (without the cost), it does not

crease badly and washes well by hand. A beautiful but expensive option is 100% silk. These silky fabrics may not appeal to everyone (the traditionalists might prefer 100% cotton), but I find that silky fabrics are far more practical, despite their delicate appearance. Cotton may appear more functional but it creases badly when washed – remember that a quilted article can never be ironed as this flattens the batting/wadding, thus making cotton unsuitable for our purposes. Polysilk, on the other hand, does not crease when cleaned according to the instructions on page 15. An added advantage of using silky fabrics is the wide range of beautiful colours to choose from.

Silky fabrics quilt better too, as polysilk is more flexible than cotton fabrics, which can be rather unyielding. The beautiful puffiness of hand quilting is lost on cotton fabrics.

Silky fabrics are not practical for all of the projects, however. The tablecloth, serviettes, tray cloths and guest towels were embroidered on cotton, a more durable and functional fabric.

Polysilk was used for the hand-quilted and candlewicked quilt, the christening robe, cream cushions and framed pictures in this book. There is a choice of smooth or crushed polysilk on the market – either one will do, depending on your preference, although crushed polysilk does add textural interest.

Satins are not suitable for any of these projects. They do not wash or wear well and fray badly. The shine of the fabric can also be rather garish. You may like to choose from other fabric types, for example, a good quality chintz (glazed cotton) or traditional calico. Remember to pre-shrink cottons or calico before using them, unlike polysilk which does not have to be pre-shrunk.

Your choice of colours depends on personal preference. However, it is a good idea to stick to neutral colours when making soft furnishings so that you can use them in any room, no matter how often you change the colour scheme. Remember, many of these projects may become heirlooms, passed from one generation to the next – and the next generation may not be fond of yellow or red!

Try to use a few different shades of the same colour, such as light, medium and darker pink for the same project. This adds an interesting dimension to the work. In the *Still Life* design (page 88), for example, five different shades of pink can be used for the flowers and the vase, while one or two shades of green can be used for the leaves.

HINTS

❖ *When using designs that include a number of circles, use smooth rather than crushed fabric. A circle on crushed fabric distorts when the fabric is pulled taut in the hoop. If, however, you prefer to use a crushed fabric for a circular design, pull the fabric square taut in the hoop before pinning and drawing the design onto the fabric. Place the fabric and the hoop against a window or light-box which will allow the pattern to show through the fabric (see Pin the pattern to the background, page 24, and Trace the design onto the background block, page 26).*

❖ *Avoid dark shades if planning an heirloom. A good idea when using primary colours is to use the duskier shades (as in a Persian rug) which always tone-in well.*

How much fabric do I purchase?

❖ A rough guideline is four blocks per 1.25 m (1¼ yds) for a cushion or a quilt *(figs. 2a and 2b)*.

❖ For a cushion, you will need a 57 x 57 cm (22½ x 22½ in) square block for the front and roughly a 60 cm

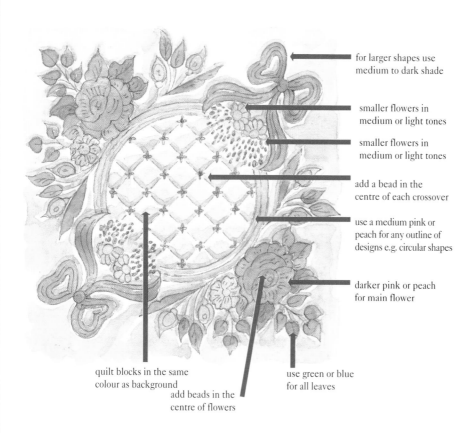

for larger shapes use
medium to dark shade

smaller flowers in
medium or light tones

smaller flowers in
medium or light tones

add a bead in the
centre of each crossover

use a medium pink or
peach for any outline of
designs e.g. circular shapes

darker pink or peach
for main flower

quilt blocks in the same
colour as background

add beads in the
centre of flowers

use green or blue
for all leaves

FIG. 3 MONTE CARLO PATTERN

(24 in) strip for the backing, therefore approximately 1.25·m (1¹/4 yds) per cushion for the front and the back.

❖ For a quilt, first work out how many blocks you will require (*see* page 42, *Calculating how many blocks for a quilt*). Divide the number of blocks required by two (you should be able to fit two blocks across the width of the fabric) and multiply by 57 cm (22¹/2 in), for example: 12 blocks for a double bed divided by 2 x 57 cm (22¹/2 in) = 3.42 m (1.35 yds).

❖ Refer to the projects in this book for details on buying fabric.

Which threads and colours should I use?

Using coloured embroidery threads and silk ribbon adds depth and looks more interesting than the cream-on-cream look we have become used to.

The best thread to use for fine and intricate designs is a six-strand skein of coloured embroidery thread.

Silk ribbon, which is a relatively new thread on the market, has also been introduced in some of the designs. Silk ribbon is 3-4 mm (¹/8 in) wide and the texture and colour it adds to a design is very attractive and effective. As the colour range for silk ribbon is not that extensive, use silk ribbon that is one shade lighter than the darkest pink, peach, green or blue thread.

When making up the quarter designs or the smaller designs, an important guideline for colour is as follows (whether embroidering the design or combining fabric shapes with embroidery *(fig. 3))*:

❖ For the main or larger flowers in the design, use slightly darker pink or peach tones. Remember that the main

flowers (the larger ones) will be the most prominent part and darkest colour of the design. The smaller flowers and leaves will always be one, two or three shades lighter than the colour of the main flowers.

❖ For all the leaves, use a medium or light shade of green or blue. Do not use too dark a shade of green or blue, as the leaves will then overshadow the main flowers.

❖ For the quilted blocks in the centre of the design (indicated with a broken line), use thread the same colour as the background block. Alternatively, you may like to use a light shade of pink or peach to complement the colour of the main flowers.

❖ For any outline of the design, for example, circles or straight lines, use a medium shade of pink or peach. Too dark a shade will result in the main flowers 'disappearing'.

❖ When using fabric shapes in a design, for example, in the *Still Life* or *Shelley* designs, anchor the raw edges of the fabric shape to the background block using French or colonial knots. The thread used to make these knots

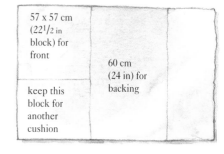

57 x 57 cm
(22¹/2 in)
block for
front

60 cm
(24 in) for
backing

keep this
block for
another
cushion

FIG. 2A 1.25 M (1¹/4 YDS) = 1 CUSHION

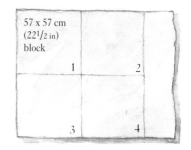

57 x 57 cm
(22¹/2 in)
block

1   2

3   4

FIG. 2B 1.25 M (1¹/4 YDS) = 4 QUILT BLOCKS

must be exactly the same colour as the fabric shapes. Always use two strands of six-strand cotton to anchor the fabric shapes along the raw edges. Never use silk ribbon to anchor them as it is far too thick.

HINTS

❖ *Remember to use only one, two or three strands of thread so that the stitches are not too clumsy for the design. If you prefer, however, traditional no. 5 or no. 8 cotton thread can be used, although it is probably too thick for delicate patterns. Stitches are sewn through all the layers of fabric, i.e. fabric, batting/wadding and muslin. For couching you may wish to use two to six strands. See Stitch codes and legends on page 20, for which colour and how many strands of thread to use for each stitch.*
❖ *Test coloured thread for colour-fastness by washing it in hot water before using it.*

Why use beads?

Beads, if used correctly, can enhance a design and they can also add a bit of fun to your work! In the same way, a design can soon look gaudy if too many beads are added. Used discreetly, beads provide an almost hidden element, as they are often not noticed at first. Use beads to form the centre of flowers or at each crossover of any quilted blocks in a design such as *Alaska*. (The quilted blocks are the dotted (broken) lines found mostly in the centre of the design. Some designs (such as the *Parasol* design) have no quilted blocks at all.)

See *Stitch codes and legends* on page 21, on how to attach a bead. Beads are indicated on each pattern by a ● or ○ for round beads and, if you are using teardrop-shaped beads, include them in the design with a ᴆ shape in places, instead of a detached chain (*see* page 18). Some designs have beads next to the flower shapes (for example,

Parasol) which form smaller 'petals' around the flower shape. Use beads which tone in with the general colour scheme, usually one shade lighter than the main flowers, or use mother-of-pearl cream, or light green.

Suitable beads to buy are glass seed beads but I also use the plastic beads found in bridal shops which give you a good colour selection.

HINT

Do not use too large a bead as this could look cumbersome and spoil the design. The only time a larger bead is suitable is for the centre of a silk ribbon daisy.

Which batting/wadding should I use?

Batting/wadding is available in various thicknesses. For cushion or quilt blocks, the thicker polyester batting/wadding is used. The 135 g (4 oz) per square or 150 g (4¹/₂ oz) is ideal. If you're not sure of the weight, judge the thickness, which is approximately 2.5 cm (1 in) thick. The batting/wadding should be soft but not too fluffy, otherwise the 'hairs' are pulled off easily.

Avoid using the rougher type of batting/wadding for the sides of the quilt – if it is too hard, the quilt will not lie smoothly against the bed. Rather use the rougher type of batting/wadding for cushions or quilt blocks.

For framed projects (*see A framed gallery* on page 55), choose the very thinnest batting/wadding you can find. I use 100 g (3¹/₂ oz) or the thinner 67 g (2 oz) batting/wadding (used for quilted jackets) for each square. Thicker batting/wadding is bulky and does not frame well unless the frame is thick and box-like.

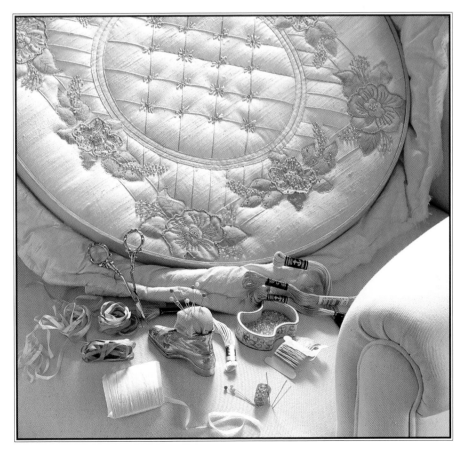

THE ENGLISH GARDEN PATTERN SHOWN HERE COMBINES CANDLEWICKING WITH FABRIC SHAPES

❖ *Batting/wadding is sold per metre (yard) and is not to be confused with the polyester stuffing or filling used to fill cushions or toys.*

❖ *Always cut the batting/wadding square 3-5 cm (1-2 in) bigger than the background block as the batting/wadding tends to 'shrink' when quilting. This will result in the batting/wadding being smaller than the fabric block and a neat finish will therefore be impossible.*

❖ *Only cut off the excess batting/wadding once the raw edge of the block has been zigzagged through all the layers (see Preparing the block for a cushion or quilt, page 35).*

❖ *It is not necessary to pre-wash polyester batting/wadding as it does not shrink.*

Why use muslin for backing the batting/wadding?

Muslin (100% cotton) is used behind the batting/wadding when embroidering and quilting as it prevents the batting/wadding 'hairs' from coming through onto the fabric side of the block as you embroider the stitches. The muslin also gives the article body, thus preventing the finished product from being too puckered. Remember to pre-wash the muslin and to cut it exactly the same size as the batting/wadding square.

It is not necessary to use muslin on the back of the batting/wadding when making framed pictures as the 'hairs' will not pull through to the fabric side of the block. It is also easier to stretch the work for framing if there are only two layers of fabric.

Which fabric is best for backing cushions and quilts?

Cushions can look most professional when the same fabric is used for both the front and the back of the cover. This, however, is a matter of choice.

Bear in mind that using a silky fabric as a backing may cause the cushion to slip off the chair or sofa more easily. Choose fabrics which are practical and wash well.

For silky and cotton quilts, I suggest that you use a good quality polyester or cotton sheet as a backing. Buy a sheet one size bigger than the quilt (for example, a king-size sheet for a double-bed quilt) so that there will be no joins in the fabric. Choose a sheet the same colour as the quilt.

I only attach the sheet once the quilt has been joined and made up as this sheet covers all the embroidery on the reverse (muslin) side of the blocks. (This means that you do not have to be too fussy about what the work looks like on the reverse side of the block!) If you find the sheet ballooning too much for your liking, use embroidery thread or silk ribbon to tie off the knots after catching each block at the corner through the sheeting onto the muslin and batting/wadding of the quilt *(fig. 3)*.

Which needles and pins should I use?

❖ It is important to use the correct needle – a needle with a small eye damages the embroidery thread, removes the sheen from the thread

and is frustrating to thread! Use a no. 9 crewel embroidery needle for six-strand thread. If you like, use a no. 9 quilting 'between' needle for the quilting stitches, but this is not essential – the embroidery needle will do.

❖ Use a no. 22 chenille needle for silk ribbon and the traditional no. 5 and no. 8 cottons. When working with silk ribbon, it is important to use a needle with a large eye. The ribbon must be flat when threaded through the eye (a folded ribbon will not result in a neat stitch).

❖ Remember to always use a sharp needle – a blunt needle will cause snags in silky fabrics.

❖ Use sharp, long steel pins with coloured heads so that no unwelcome guests are left behind! Pins tend to disappear into the batting/wadding when working on the article.

Which quilting hoop should I use and why?

A hoop is essential for this type of candlewick embroidery. The hoop allows for even tension throughout the quilted article and results in a perfectly smooth finish. I always use as large a hoop as the design allows so that I am able to embroider all or most of the stitches without having to move the hoop and thereby change the tension.

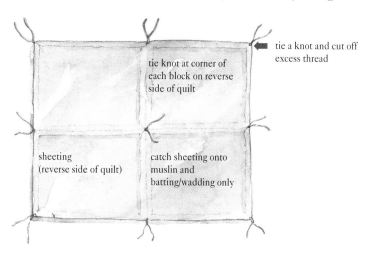

tie a knot and cut off excess thread

tie knot at corner of each block on reverse side of quilt

sheeting (reverse side of quilt)

catch sheeting onto muslin and batting/wadding only

FIG. 4

RICH COLOURS AND FABRIC SHAPES ARE USED TO MAKE UP THE MONTE CARLO PATTERN

There is no need to tack the layers together when using a hoop as they are unable to move when pulled taut in the frame.

There is a significant difference between an embroidery and a quilting hoop. A quilting hoop is thicker in order to hold all the layers together. The wood is about 2 cm (just less than an inch) thick and is tightened with a wing nut and not a screw. An embroidery hoop is much thinner than a quilting hoop. It only needs to hold one layer of fabric and the hoop is tightened by a round screw. An embroidery hoop is only used for the *Wedding Gifts* (*see* page 64).

❖ A 45.7 cm (18 in) quilting hoop is used for the cushion and quilt blocks.

❖ A 35.5 cm (14 in) quilting hoop is used for the *Framed Gallery* and *Tea Cosy*.

❖ A 25 cm (10 in) quilting hoop is used for the other smaller projects, such as the *Christening Bib* (page 60) and the *Christening Robe* (page 61).

HINTS

❖ *If you find that the design is too small for the hoop you have, cut the background block 5 cm (2 in) bigger than the size of your hoop. Do the same for the batting/wadding and muslin. Draw the design and outline of the pattern onto the centre of the fabric block, embroider and cut down to size once completed. Don't forget to draw the outline (for example, the outer square or shape of the* Christening Bib*) onto the centre of the square – it is very difficult to draw a neat shape onto the fabric once it is quilted.*

❖ *Always try to have most of the design or the whole design in the hoop. Using a hoop*

which is too small means that you will have to move it to finish the pattern and it will therefore be impossible to achieve a perfectly smooth article. The hoop can damage the embroidered stitches if it is too small and has to be moved to include the rest of the design.

Why use a pencil for tracing onto fabric?

I prefer not to use water-soluble pens for tracing, as the tips of these pens are too thick for these designs. I usually use a medium to soft lead pencil (an HB or B pencil). Lightly drawn onto the fabric, the pencil lines disappear into the quilted folds as you quilt and are covered by the knots or stem stitching as you sew. As the pencil lines do not fade, wash out or rub out once drawn, it is very important to draw neatly, lightly, and to use a sharp pencil to make thin, fine lines. Use a ruler to draw straight lines as a hand-drawn crooked line cannot be rubbed out.

HINT
Pencils with lead refills are ideal as the lead requires no sharpening and draws a fine, sharp line. The lead is available in HB or B – I normally use the B lead but the choice is up to you.

What other equipment or materials are needed?

❖ A clean steam iron or an iron with a protective cover to prevent scorching (remember to always set it on the correct temperature, i.e. silk setting for silk, and so on)

❖ transparent tape

❖ 45-50 cm (18-20 in) ruler

❖ a sharp pair of dressmakers' scissors and a small, sharp pair of embroidery scissors

❖ sewing machine with zig-zag stitch (if possible) – use an 80 or 90 Universal needle for all projects

❖ sunny window or a glass table with a light underneath it for tracing

❖ 3B pencil for tracing onto Vilene or fusible webbing only

❖ HB or B pencil for tracing the pattern onto the fabric

❖ black fineliner pen – the line must be clear once photocopied

❖ several A4 sheets of tracing paper

❖ leather or steel thimble (optional)

❖ polyester filling if making cushions

❖ a soft glue stick if using fabric shapes (*see* page 29) (a glue stick is not a liquid glue – liquid glue will mark the fabric)

❖ iron-on Vilene or fusible webbing if using fabric shapes (*see Making the fabric shapes* on page 29)

❖ T-square to draw blocks

❖ fabric for frill, binding or cording if making a cushion (*see* individual projects which begin on page 35).

HANDY HINTS WHEN CANDLE-WICKING AND QUILTING

1. Use the best quality fabrics you can afford to ensure heirloom quality. Avoid using poor quality fabrics for the backs of cushions.

2. To determine a good finish, trace the pattern as neatly and precisely as possible. Join carefully. Draw the pattern onto the fabric accurately, using a ruler to draw straight lines.

3. When making a quilt, draw the required size square onto a cardboard sheet and make a template so that each fabric square will be exactly the same size.

4. Always cut batting/wadding and muslin squares 3-5 cm (1-2 in) bigger than the fabric block. Batting/wadding 'shrinks' as you quilt and if there is any excess, it can be cut off later.

5. Cut the background fabric block at least 5-8 cm (2-3 in) bigger than the hoop you will be using. Draw the required block size and design onto the centre of the fabric square and only cut to the required size once complete.

6. Keep the layers of batting/wadding and fabric taut in the hoop at all times. Tighten every time you pick up your work to ensure a smooth finish.

7. Never iron quilted articles as the heat from the iron flattens the batting/wadding and all the quilting disappears.

8. Never store fabrics in plastic. They will sweat and discolour. Rather wrap them in an old sheet or pillowcase. Do not fold; rather keep flat or gently rolled up. Store moth-repellents separately in fabric. Remember that hand-crafted articles are best 'stored' on display in your home.

9. Always pre-wash cotton fabrics to remove any remaining printing dyes. Slight shrinkage occurs with cotton fabrics and blends.

10. Before placing the fabric layers in the hoop, make sure that they are perfectly smooth. Press the fabric on the wrong side to remove any creases (it cannot be ironed once quilted).

11. Remember to empty the water from your steam iron after use to prevent rust marks being made on the fabric. Test the iron on a scrap of cloth before pressing.

12. Always iron on the wrong side of the fabric. Before pressing, set the iron to the correct temperature – for polysilk and taffeta, use the silk setting.

13. A commercial spray starch, available in a can, keeps the article flat while pressing, especially when pressing backing slips for cushions or making bias binding for quilts.

14. If your iron becomes coated with glue from Vilene or spray starch, there is a hot iron cleaner on the market which removes the residue.

15. When filling cushion pads, make sure that the pad is well-filled but not so that the cover puckers along the edges. Down is an expensive, but environmentally friendly alternative, to polyester filling.

16. If you prefer to use quilting cotton instead of two strands of embroidery thread, run the quilting cotton through beeswax to prevent soiling and the thread from knotting. Use only one strand of this cotton .

17. Change the needle on your sewing machine regularly. A blunt needle will cause the thread to snap and may snag threads on silky fabrics. Use an 80 or 90 Universal needle.

18. To develop fine embroidery skills takes time, patience and practice. Don't be deterred by imperfections – the designs are detailed enough to hide most 'mistakes'! Do not unpick unless absolutely necessary – the charm of your article may be lost if it looks too perfect.

A GUIDE TO MATTRESS SIZES

A guide to approximate mattress sizes is given below. Please measure your mattress before beginning a quilt.

TWIN OR SINGLE BED MATTRESS
92 cm x 190 cm (3 ft x 6 ft 3 in)

THREE-QUARTER BED MATTRESS
110 cm x 190 cm (3 ft 5 in x 6 ft 3 in)

DOUBLE BED MATTRESS
150 cm x 190 cm (4 ft 6 in x 6 ft 3 in)

QUEEN-SIZE BED MATTRESS (NOT UK)
153 cm x 190 cm (5 ft x 6 ft 3 in)

KING-SIZE BED MATTRESS
180 cm x 190 cm (5 ft x 6 ft 3 in)

EXTRA-LONG KING-SIZE BED MATTRESS
180 cm x 200 cm (5 ft 10 in x 6 ft 7 in)

WASHING INSTRUCTIONS

Wiping an article

Before washing a soiled article, rather consider wiping the article first. Polysilks are easily wiped clean and I always clean my cushions, quilts and wall-hangings this way. Wiping instead of washing gives the article a longer life span. It is important, however, to follow these steps carefully to prevent watermarks forming.

1. Take a clean, damp face-cloth and a white soap bar.
2. Lather the face-cloth as if bathing.
3. Wring out excess soap and water until the cloth is damp, not wet.
4. Wipe the block or quilt block to remove the mark first.
5. Do not stop there, but continue to wipe the entire block or quilt block so that the whole block is damp. This prevents any watermarks forming.
6. Place in the sun to dry quickly to prevent watermarks forming.

HINTS

❖ *If a watermark has formed once the article has dried, repeat steps 1-6.*
❖ *Cottons do not wipe well. Wash stained cottons as the stains tend to set in cotton.*

THIS CUSHION (FANTASY PATTERN) ADDS ELEGANCE TO ANY ROOM

Washing an article

1. First test all the fabrics used in the quilt for colour fastness. Use a few damp, white paper napkins and gently rub each colour with the napkin. If there is colour on the napkin, do not wash the quilt.
2. If washing a cushion, remove the cushion pad from the cushion cover.
3. Place the article in a basin or bath of cool or tepid water (*not* hot water) to which mild soap flakes have been added. Make sure that the soap flakes have dissolved in the water first, otherwise they may leave marks.
4. Soak for a few minutes, then rub the soiled area gently with your finger-tips to remove the marks. If washing a quilt, fill the bath so that the entire quilt can be soaked.
5. Drain the water from the basin or bath.
6. Set the article aside or simply move it to the other end of the bath and refill the basin or bath with cool water. Soak the article for a few minutes to remove the soap. If washing a quilt, continue soaking and rinsing until the water is clean.
7. Drain the water and gently pat the article dry between two towels, keeping it flat at all times. Do not wring. If washing a quilt, drain the water and using several towels, pat gently to remove as much water as possible before removing from the bath.
8. Dry in a shady area. Peg cushions by two of the corners. Hang the quilt over two or three strands of washing line so it is evenly spread.
9. Choose a hot or windy day so that the articles dry quickly to prevent watermarks forming.
10. If it is absolutely necessary to iron the article, place the steam iron close to the fabric but do not touch it, and allow the steam to iron out the creases.

EMBROIDERY STITCHES

The American pioneer women originally used French knots, satin stitch and back stitch, and then progressed to using colonial knots, chain stitch and stem stitch. Newcomers to candlewick embroidery, as well as the more experienced students, are attracted by the simple and effective stitches used which are quick and easy, and require little expertise. The designs in this book are fairly detailed, so it is unnecessary to use elaborate and time consuming embroidery stitches. The design, not the stitches, determines the appearance of the finished article. In this chapter I've described the stitches which are used most often in candlewick embroidery.

We *begin* all stitches by making a knot in the thread, rather than a back stitch (thread is expensive and making a knot is a more economical way to begin) – the article may not be as neat at the back as it would be by doing a back stitch, but no-one usually sees the back anyway! You may, however, prefer to start with a few back stitches; the choice is yours.

Silk ribbon cannot be started with a knot as the knot would be too large and bulky. Leave a 2.5 cm (1 in) tail when starting with silk ribbon and catch the tail as you make the second or third stitch.

To *end off* embroidery threads where there are two to six strands, separate the strands to make two threads. Make five to eight knots, one on top of the other, with the threads. As an alternative, make a few back stitches, one on top of the other, instead of making a knot, or run the thread underneath the adjoining stitches to end off.

To end off silk ribbon, catch the tail end of the ribbon when making the next stitch, or back stitch by inserting the needle through the tail end of the ribbon into the backing and batting/wadding to secure it.

See Using silk ribbon on page 28 for how to thread a chenille needle with silk ribbon.

STITCH GUIDES

1. Quilting or running stitch

❖ SEWN THROUGH ALL LAYERS.

Use two strands of embroidery thread. Push the needle through all the layers of the fabric 'sandwich' *(fig. 1a)*. Use up and down stab stitches (*see* Note below for instructions). The stitches must be 2-3 mm long (or 8, 10 or 12 stitches per inch) and spaced evenly. *Pull tight* to form a gully.

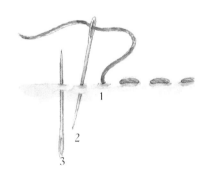

FIG. 1A QUILTING/RUNNING STITCH

NOTE

Stab stitches simply mean that only half or one stitch is made at a time (fig. 1b).

2. Back stitch

❖ SEWN THROUGH ALL LAYERS.

Use two strands of embroidery thread. Back stitch is useful for defining lines of small curves. *Pull tight* as for the quilting stitch *(fig. 2)*.

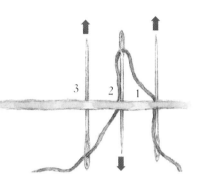

FIG. 1B STAB STITCH

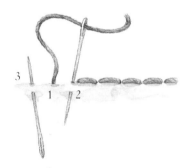

FIG. 2 BACK STITCH

3. Stem stitch

❖ SEWN THROUGH ALL LAYERS.

Use one or two strands of embroidery thread (one strand for very fine detail). As for the quilting or running stitch, bring the needle up from the back of the work along the drawn line on the fabric. Make a running stitch and pull the thread taut to the back of the work. Re-insert the needle half way back, pulling the thread taut to the front. This is also a 'stab stitch' (*see* Note on this page). Thus, for this type of quilted stem stitch, a normal running stitch is made on the fabric (top) side of the work and a back stitch is made on the muslin and batting/wadding (back) side of the work *(fig. 3a)*.

Bring the needle up on the widest part of the curve, i.e. on the outside of the curve *(fig. 3b)*. On a straight line, it does not matter on which side of the stitch you bring out the needle and the thread.

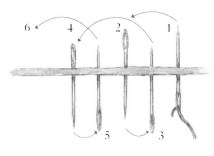

FIG. 3A STEM STITCH

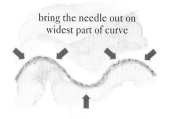

bring the needle out on widest part of curve

FIG. 3B STEM STITCH

4. Chain stitch

❖ SEWN THROUGH ONLY THE TOP LAYER OF THE FABRIC AND PART OF THE BATTING/WADDING.

Use two strands of embroidery thread. Bring the needle from the back at the starting point of the chain *(fig. 4)*. Make a loop with the thread. The needle returns to the place where the thread emerged, and the thread loops underneath the needle.

Bring the needle out at the opposite curve of the chain and, making sure that the thread is still looped, gently pull to form a chain. Insert the needle back into the previous chain.

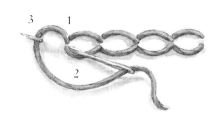

FIG. 4 CHAIN STITCH

5. French knot and French knot filling

❖ SEWN THROUGH ALL LAYERS.

Use one or two strands of embroidery thread (one strand for very fine detail).

Bring the needle from the back of the fabric to the front *(fig. 5)*. Wind the thread around the needle three times. Push the needle back through the fabric, close to the point where it was brought through the first time.

Pull the thread while the needle is still in the fabric and the batting/wadding, and pull it down onto the fabric until the knot rests tightly on the fabric. At the same time, pull the thread slightly to tighten the knot around the needle.

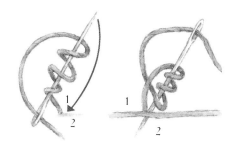

FIG. 5 FRENCH KNOT

Hold the thread taut with your free hand. Now pull the needle to the back of the work, pulling gently on the thread at the back of the work until the knot lies neatly on the fabric. Insert the needle from the back to the next dot, pulling the thread to the top of the work. Pull the thread taut

and keep it taut while winding it around the needle for the next knot. This prevents the previous knot from being too loose. For larger dots use silk ribbon wound once around the needle. You can use French knots to fill a shape. Make the knots close together to form the shape. You may like to outline the shape with stem stitch first.

6. Detached chain

❖ SEWN THROUGH ONLY THE TOP LAYER OF FABRIC AND PART OF THE BATTING/WADDING. THE ANCHORING STITCH, HOWEVER, IS MADE THROUGH ALL THE LAYERS. In a detached chain, each stitch is held down separately with the thread you are working with.

Use silk ribbon where a larger teardrop ⎛ is drawn. Use two strands of embroidery thread where a smaller teardrop ⎝ is drawn. Make a single chain as for the chain stitch *(fig. 4)* but anchor each shape by inserting the needle to the back of the work 2 mm (1/16 in) away from the rounded part of the chain *(fig. 6)*. Do not pull too taut or the chain will close. A chain made from silk ribbon should look like a petal that has fallen onto the fabric (not too loose or too tight).

HINT

For an interesting variation, make the anchor stitch a little longer and you will form an attractive bell-like stitch.

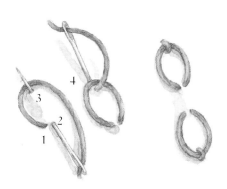

FIG. 6 DETACHED CHAIN/LAZY DAISY

7. Lazy daisy

❖ SEWN ONLY THROUGH THE TOP LAYER OF FABRIC AND PART OF THE BATTING/ WADDING. THE ANCHORING STITCH, HOW- EVER, IS MADE THROUGH ALL THE LAYERS.

Use two strands of embroidery thread or, for a larger daisy, use silk ribbon.

Follow the same procedure as for the detached chain, but form the loops into a flower. Add a bead to the centre so that it looks like a daisy.

8. Colonial knot

❖ SEWN THROUGH ALL LAYERS.

A colonial knot is slightly bigger than a French knot and can be used instead of one. Use one or two strands of embroidery thread or silk ribbon.

Bring the needle through the back of the fabric to the front, just left of the dot indicating where the knot is to be made *(fig. 7)*. Hold the embroidery thread lightly between your thumb and forefinger. Push the needle under the thread from left to right, then twist the thread over and under the point of the needle to form a figure of eight. Insert the needle through the fabric to the right of where the needle first emerged, pulling the needle and thread firmly to the back of the fabric and tightening as for a French knot. Continue in this way, bringing the needle through to the right of the next dot.

9. Satin stitch

❖ SEWN THROUGH ALL LAYERS.

Use two strands of embroidery thread. This can be used as an alternative fill- ing stitch although it can be difficult to keep tidy – rather use a French knot filling. Satin stitch consists of straight, even stitches worked closely together *(fig. 8)*. For a neater result, begin satin stitch at the widest point of the area that is to be covered and work towards the edge. Turn the work around to complete the uncovered part. The stitches must not overlap. Be careful

DETAIL OF THE ROSE GARLAND PATTERN SHOWING CANDLEWICKING AND FABRIC SHAPES

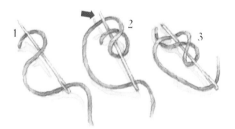

FIG. 7 COLONIAL KNOT

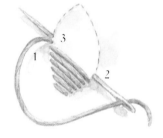

FIG. 8 SATIN STITCH

that you do not pull the thread so tight- ly that the fabric puckers. Finish off by running the needle under several stitches at the back of the article.

10. Extended French knot

❖ SEWN THROUGH ALL LAYERS.

Silk ribbon is ideal for this stitch. It is thick and thus creates very effective 'petals' when the flower is formed *(fig. 9)*. Follow the same procedure as for a French knot but instead of insert- ing the needle back where the thread first came through, insert it 3-4 mm (1/8 in) away from the thread. When using embroidery thread, wind it three

times around the needle. When using silk ribbon, wind it once around the needle. Make four, five or six petals to form a daisy. Use embroidery thread to attach a bead in the centre of the daisy.

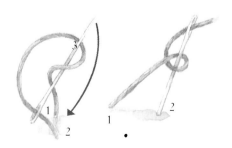

FIG. 9 EXTENDED FRENCH KNOT

11. Couching

❖ TWO TO SIX STRANDS OF THREAD LIE LOOSELY ON TOP OF THE FABRIC. ONE TO TWO STRANDS ANCHOR THIS THREAD THROUGH ALL THE LAYERS.

Couching is used for outlining or filling. Thicker strands of thread to be couched are laid on the surface of the material and held in place with small, straight couching stitches using a thinner thread.

Depending on the detail of the design, use two to six strands of thread and a no. 22 chenille needle for the thicker (laid) thread. Cut the thread 1 m (1 yd) long and thread it through the chenille needle. Make a knot at the long end. To anchor the laid threads, use only one to two strands of a shorter thread, about 40 cm (16 in) long, in the same colour, and an embroidery needle. Make a knot in this shorter thread. Bring the laid threads from the back of the fabric to the front of the fabric. Allow the threads to lie loosely on the drawn line *(fig. 10)*.

Bring the shorter couching thread from the back of the fabric to the front, 3 mm (1/8 in) from where the laid thread came through. Stitch or anchor the laid thread in place by inserting the embroidery needle back over and under the laid thread. Space these stitches about 3 mm (1/8 in) apart and sew the laid thread along the drawn line. Pull the laid thread taut while you sew so that it lies evenly along the drawn line, with no kinks in the thread.

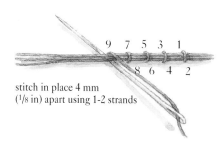

stitch in place 4 mm (1/8 in) apart using 1-2 strands

FIG. 10 COUCHING

For filling in flower stems, for example, first outline stems with couching as above, then insert the needle from the back and bring it up next to the outline, filling up spaces in between with couching so that there are no gaps between stitches.

12. Whipped or raised couching

❖ SEWN ONLY UNDERNEATH THE COUCHED TWO TO SIX-STRAND THREADS.

After stitching the two or six-strand threads along the drawn line, re-thread the chenille needle with two to six-strands of matching embroidery thread. Cut the thread 1 m (1 yd) long.

Insert the blunt side of the needle under and over each segment of the couched thread *(fig. 11)*. The fabric is not sewn at all.

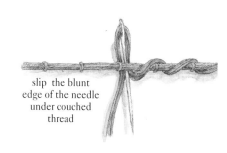

slip the blunt edge of the needle under couched thread

FIG. 11 WHIPPED COUCHING

13. Attaching a bead

❖ SEWN THROUGH ALL LAYERS.

Use two strands of embroidery thread. Attach bead by running the thread once or twice through the eye of the bead, as you would when sewing on a 'one-eyed' button *(fig. 12)*.

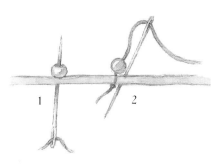

FIG. 12 ATTACHING A BEAD

14. Honeycomb stitch

❖ WOVEN STITCHES LIE LOOSELY ON TOP OF THE FABRIC AND ARE ANCHORED AT THE INTERSECTIONS THROUGH ALL THE LAYERS.

This is another form of couching and is a useful stitch in an area that requires heavy shading, for example, the centre of a flower. It is not suitable for large areas, however – rather use plain couching *(see Couching)*. Use two strands of embroidery thread and an embroidery needle *(fig. 13)*.

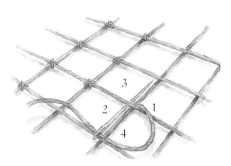

FIG. 13 HONEYCOMB STITCH

STITCH CODES AND LEGENDS

The stitches to use for each design are indicated by the use of lines:

❖ A solid line denotes that stem, back, couching or honeycomb stitch can be used (any of these are suitable).
❖ A broken line indicates quilting or running stitch.
❖ Dots indicate French or colonial knots and beads.
❖ Teardrops indicate a detached chain. A teardrop bead can also be used where small teardrops are indicated.

These stitch codes and legends are merely guidelines. Be as creative as you wish and use different stitches wherever you choose.

The colour combinations are also only suggestions, but I would suggest that you do not stray too far from these guidelines.

STITCH	ALTERNATIVE	PATTERN CODE	COLOUR
QUILTING (use embroidery thread – two strands)	Back stitch Stem stitch Couching Chain stitch	------------------- Broken line	For background quilting, e.g. centre blocks in the design, use cream or a complementary shade. Use green or colour of leaves to quilt around the fabric shapes to anchor them to the background.
STEM STITCH (use embroidery thread – two strands)	Chain stitch Back stitch Couching Quilting	~~~~~~~~ Solid line	Use darkest pink or peach to embroider main flower shapes. Use green to embroider leaf shapes and veins. Use medium to dark shades to embroider the outline of the design.
FRENCH KNOTS (use embroidery thread – one or two strands, or silk ribbon)	Colonial knots Beads	o ∴ oo .	Use a slightly darker or the shade that matches fabric flowers for their centres (if using beads, use one shade lighter). Anchor fabric shapes to the background with knots. Use darker shades of pink or peach to form the flower if not using fabric shapes. Use pink, peach or green silk ribbon to make knots where there is a large o.
EXTENDED FRENCH KNOT (use silk ribbon or embroidery thread – one or two strands)	Lazy daisy	❋ ❋ ❋	Silk – pink (light) or peach. Embroidery thread – pink (medium or light) or peach.
COUCHING (use embroidery thread – two to six strands)	Quilting Back stitch Satin stitch	~~~~~~~~ Solid line	Use medium pink or peach for outline stitch. Use green for flower stems.
HONEYCOMB STITCH (use embroidery thread – two strands)	Back stitch Stem stitch Quilting	▦▦▦▦ Usually found in centre of flowers	Use darker shades of pink/peach to match flower shapes.
CHAIN STITCH (use embroidery thread – two strands)	French knots sewn close together Couching Stem stitch Quilting	A solid line or ∞∞∞∞∞ chain	Use medium pink or peach for outline shapes, e.g. circles or green for stems of flowers.
DETACHED CHAIN AND LAZY DAISY (use embroidery thread – two strands, or silk ribbon)	Extended French knot Teardrop bead	❦ For small teardrops use two strands embroidery thread ❧ For larger teardrops for leaves use silk ribbon ❋ ❋ ❋ Lazy daisy – use embroidery cotton	Use green, yellow or pink/peach for smaller teardrops. Use green, yellow, peach, light pink, lavender or light blue for larger teardrops (if you want to use medium shade of ribbon, use it sparingly). Use medium or light pink or peach.
FRENCH KNOT FILLING (use embroidery thread – two strands)	Satin stitch Couching	⚘ Smaller buds · ❀ To make rose or flower shapes	Use medium or dark thread to fill a shape.

CANDLEWICKING AND QUILTING STEP-BY-STEP

These basic steps will guide the most inexperienced needlewoman through the different stages of candlewicking and quilting, and will be followed for all of the projects. The Wedding Gifts, however, are not quilted through the various layers of fabric and are explained in that section.

WHAT DO I NEED?

The exact material requirements are given under each project. Familiarize yourself with the following points before you start:

1. PATTERNS *See How do I trace and join the quarter patterns?*, page 7.
2. BACKGROUND FABRIC *See Which fabrics and colours should I choose?*, page 9.
3. BATTING/WADDING *See Which batting/wadding should I use?*, page 11.
4. MUSLIN *See Why use muslin for backing the batting/wadding?*, page 12.
5. EMBROIDERY THREADS *See Which threads and colours should I use?*, page 10. A *rough* guide to how many skeins of thread or how much silk ribbon to purchase is as follows:

Thread/ribbon requirements (per block)

For cushion and quilt blocks, an average requirement is four or five different coloured skeins of thread. Please refer to each of the smaller projects for the number of skeins and colours to purchase.

Colours of embroidery thread

The following threads are required:
– a light, medium and dark peach or pink for the flowers;
– one shade of green or blue for the leaves. The green must be a shade lighter than the darkest pink or peach so as not to dominate the design;

– one shade to match the background block, for example, cream for cream, to quilt any blocks in the centre of the design. If there are no quilted blocks in the centre of the design (for example, the framed pictures or the *Parasol* design), it is not necessary to purchase a shade to match the background cloth.

Silk ribbon

Silk ribbon 3.5-4 mm (1/8 in) wide is recommended. The wider 7 mm (1/4 in) is a little clumsy for these designs. If you do use the wider silk ribbon, use it sparingly!

– approximately 2-4 m (2-4¹/4 yds) each of two different shades in light pink or peach;
– approximately 3-5 m (3-5¹/2 yds) of light green.

6. BEADS *See Why use beads?*, page 11. Purchase beads in one or two different complementary shades.
7. FABRIC If combining candlewicking with fabric leaf and flower shapes, *see Combining candlewicking with fabric shapes*, page 29.
8. VILENE Iron-on Vilene or fusible webbing if making fabric shapes.
9. SEWING AIDS *See Which needles and pins should I use?*, page 12, *Which quilting hoop should I use and why?*, page 12, *Why use a pencil for tracing onto the fabric?*, page 13, and *What other equipment or materials are needed?*, page 14.

HINT
Buy extra meterage (yardage) if using more silk ribbon in your design.

ASSEMBLING THE PROJECT

1. Pre-wash 100% cotton fabrics to remove excess printing dyes and because slight shrinkage will occur.
❖ Soak cottons in cold water overnight to remove excess starch (*fig. 1a*). Do not to use washing powder or fabric softener – the fabric below the water will fade, while the fabric above the water will not.
❖ Soak in hot water to remove excess dye and to pre-shrink (*fig. 1b*).
❖ Press the fabric once it is dry.

soak cotton overnight in cold water to remove starch

FIG. 1A

soak cotton in hot water to remove excess dye and to pre-shrink

FIG. 1B

FIG. 2A

FIG. 2B

2. Make a tracing of the pattern and join.

❖ *See How do I trace and join the quarter patterns?*, page 7.

❖ The first 17 projects and the *Tea Cosy* (*see* page 55) are quarter patterns or half patterns. They will be copied and joined as indicated on the design (*fig. 2a*).

The *Still Life* and *Shelley* designs, and all the other smaller designs, do not need joining, but you will still have to trace or copy the patterns from the book (*fig. 2b*).

3. Cut out the background fabric.

❖ Refer to *Which fabrics and colours do I choose?*, page 9 and *How much fabric do I purchase?*, page 9.

❖ A rough guideline is to work on a 57 x 57 cm (22^1/$_2$ x 22^1/$_2$ in) block for a cushion block or a quilt block, and a 50 x 50 cm (20 x 20 in) or 30 x 30 cm (12 x 12 in) fabric block for the smaller projects which will be cut down to size once embroidered (*figs. 3a and 3b*).

Please see each individual project for how large a background block you will need.

HINTS

❖ *If you are using strong colours for your project, such as red, navy or black, add a little salt to the water to preserve the colours while washing.*

❖ *Do not wash the batting/wadding and Vilene or fusible webbing. It is also not necessary to pre-wash polyesters as these do not shrink.*

TO MAKE A CUSHION BLOCK

a. Cut a 57 x 57 cm (22^1/$_2$ x 22 ^{1}/$_2$ in) fabric block (this fits nicely into a 45.7 cm (18 in) quilting hoop).

b. Inside this fabric block, draw a 42 x 42 cm (16^1/$_2$ x 16^1/$_2$ in) square. This will be the zig-zag and cutting line later. Do not cut along this inside line at this stage as the fabric must fit snugly into the 45.7 cm (18 in) quilting hoop.

TO MAKE A QUILT BLOCK

a. Cut a 57 x 57 cm (22^1/$_2$ x 22^1/$_2$ in) fabric block (this fits nicely into a 45.7 cm (18 in) hoop).

b. DRAW THE FOLLOWING SQUARES INSIDE THIS BLOCK:

❖ For a single, double or standard king-size quilt, draw a 50 cm (20 in) square.

❖ For a queen-size or extra-long king-size quilt, draw a 55 cm (21^1/$_2$ in) square.

❖ Use a sharp HB or B pencil to draw the lines onto the fabric.

❖ Use a T-square to ensure perfect corners.

❖ Make a cardboard template for the quilt as each block needs to be exactly the same size. *See Handy Hints* number 3, page 14. You will need a 57 x 57 cm (22^1/$_2$ x 22 ^{1}/$_2$ in) template to draw and cut the fabric block, and a 50 cm (20 in) or 55 cm (21^1/$_2$ in) template to draw the inside square. When drawing the inside square on the fabric block, make sure that the square is in the centre of the fabric with equal borders – this will ensure that the design fits well into the 45.7 cm (18 in) hoop.

c. PIN THE PATTERN TO THE BACK-GROUND AS FOLLOWS:

WHEN USING LIGHTER COLOURED BACK-GROUND FABRICS (figs. 4a and 4b):

❖ Take the paper pattern and make sure it is square – cut off any excess paper from the quarter designs. Use a ruler to measure the distance. It must be equal on all four sides (from the edge of the design to the edge of the paper). For page-size designs, the pattern must be placed in the centre of

FIG. 3A CUSHION

FIG. 3B QUILT

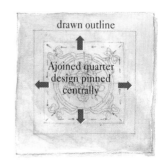

FIG. 4A

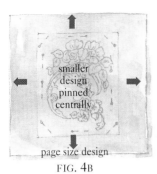

FIG. 4B

the page, i.e. if the design is not in the centre of the page, cut off any excess paper so that it is centred and the edges are equidistant from the design.

❖ Place the background fabric right side up on top of the right side of the pattern.

❖ A cream silky background will allow the design to show through.

❖ Position the pattern so that it is in the centre of the block. Use a ruler to measure that the fabric that overlaps the pattern on all four sides is equal.

❖ Pin the pattern to the fabric at the four corners and along the sides. It is important that the fabric lies flat. Make sure that folds are not formed in the fabric as you pin.

WHEN USING DARKER BACKGROUND OR COTTON FABRICS:

❖ Where the design does not show through the fabric, try taping the pattern and fabric to a sunny window or to a glass table with a light underneath. The design should show through. Pin in place as above.

❖ If using very dark fabric, where the design does not show through at all, trace the design onto tracing paper. Join four page size (A4) sheets of tracing paper together to make a size large enough for the pattern to fit onto. Pin the tracing on top of the right side of the fabric. Slip dressmakers' carbon paper underneath the tracing. Use a ballpoint pen to press the design and carbon onto the fabric.

THE RAMBLING ROSE PATTERN IS TRACED ONTO A DARK BACKGROUND FABRIC

lightly trace design onto fabric

drawn 42 cm (16 in), 50 cm (20 in),
55 cm (21¹/2 in) line.

fabric cut 57 x 57 cm (22¹/2 in)

FIG. 5

d. TRACE THE DESIGN ONTO THE
BACKGROUND BLOCK:

❖ Refer to *Why use a pencil for tracing
onto fabric?*, page 13.

❖ Take a sharp HB or B pencil (medium to soft lead) and *lightly* and neatly, trace the detail of the pattern onto
the fabric *(fig. 5)*.

❖ Draw in all the detail and use a
ruler for any straight lines. The tracing of the design is the most important step for a professional finish. The
neater you trace, the neater the finished design!

❖ Remove the pins and paper pattern.

HINTS

❖ *Use a T-square to draw perfect corners,
or cut out a cardboard template, ideal
when making cushion or quilt blocks.*

❖ *To ensure that the fabric is perfectly
smooth on the pattern, do not pick up the
fabric and pattern as you pin. Keep both*

flat on the table and slide the pin into the
fabric. If you are using a window to allow
the design to show through the fabric, you
will need to pin the centre of the pattern
firmly so that the fabric cannot move when
tracing. Using a glass table with a light
underneath means that the pattern and
fabric block lie flat and you will therefore
not need to pin anywhere near the centre of
the design.

❖ *I prefer not to press folds into the fabric
to find the centre point. These folds tend to
distort the patterns, especially any circular
shapes on a design, and a perfectly
embroidered design then becomes impossible. By measuring equal distances from
the edge of the design to the edge of the
drawn fabric square, you will be able to
find the centre point (i.e. to pin the fabric
centrally onto the pattern).*

❖ *Draw lightly, as the pencil marks will
be more prominent when placed against
the batting/wadding in the hoop.*

❖ *Do not draw a double line if you have
made a mistake. Leave the fault – it will
not be all that noticeable, but a double line
will be.*

❖ *Pencil cannot be rubbed out, washed
out and does not fade with time. The fine
pencil line is covered by the stitches and
'disappears' into the quilted folds.*

❖ *Do not draw a very thick line as the
pencil will show where the stitches have not
covered the line.*

❖ *When tracing centre blocks from the
quarter patterns, use a ruler and, where
lines do not match perfectly on the joined
pattern, use the ruler to make perfect
squares. Always use a ruler to draw a
straight line!*

❖ *When tracing circular shapes, do not
draw a solid line. Take your time and
rather draw dots or dashes to trace the
circle onto the fabric. It is very difficult to
draw a perfect circle using a solid line.*

❖ *To preserve patterns, store them in
plastic sleeves – this will enable you to use
them many times over.*

EMBROIDERING THE DESIGN

1. PLACE THE LAYERS OF BACK-
GROUND FABRIC SQUARES, BATTING/
WADDING AND MUSLIN INTO THE HOOP
(*SEE Which quilting hoop should I use and
why?*, PAGE 12) AS FOLLOWS *(fig. 6a)*:

❖ If the fabric block is smaller than
the batting/wadding, muslin and
hoop, add 6 cm (¹/4 in) strips of fabric
to enlarge it so that it fits snugly into
the hoop *(fig. 6b)*.

❖ Take the muslin square and place it
flat on a table.

❖ Lay the batting/wadding square on
top of the muslin. If your batting/
wadding has one rough and one smooth
side, place the rough side against the
muslin.

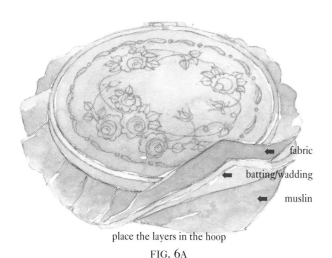

fabric
batting/wadding
muslin

place the layers in the hoop

FIG. 6A

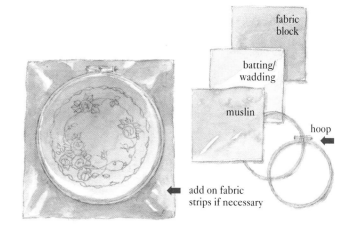

fabric
block

batting/
wadding

muslin

hoop

add on fabric
strips if necessary

FIG. 6B

A QUILTING HOOP (HOLDING THE PARASOL PATTERN) IS PORTABLE, ENABLING YOU TO EMBROIDER ALMOST ANYWHERE

❖ Centre the background fabric on top of the batting/wadding, smoothing out the creases.

❖ Take the hoop and place the three layers of fabric 'sandwich' into it as follows:

– centre the inner ring of the hoop under the muslin;

– unscrew the wing nut to enlarge the outer frame;

– centre the outer ring of the hoop on top of the fabric square to fit over the inner ring which is underneath the muslin;

– push the outer ring over the inner ring (you may need a third hand here to help you, or work on the floor using your knee as the third 'hand');

– tighten the wing nut halfway and gently stretch the top fabric until it is perfectly smooth, like a drum;

– stretch the muslin at the back as above (never pull on the batting/ wadding as it will tear);

– the fabrics should now be smooth but not so tightly stretched that the design is distorted

– tighten the wing nut firmly;

– roll and pin or tack the four corners so that they are out of the way. Do not pin anywhere inside the inner fabric square, but rather pin on the outer square of fabric. The pins may damage the fabric and, if you live near the coast, the pins may rust.

HINTS

❖ *It is important to make sure that any creases in the background fabric are ironed out before placing the layers in the hoop. Remember that a quilted article cannot be pressed later.*

❖ *It is not necessary to tack the three layers together when using a hoop. The layers cannot move in the hoop once the wing nut is tightened. Tacking also prevents a perfectly smooth finish as it tends to crease the top layer of fabric.*

❖ *The layers tend to loosen as you work, so remember, every time you pick up the hoop to tighten all the layers by gently pulling at the folded corners (the batting/wadding will not tear this way). Also pull gently at the sides of the top fabric. Perfectly smooth fabric, pulled taut in the hoop at all times, ensures a well-finished, attractive article.*

❖ *As you work, you may find it easier to rest a section of the hoop on the edge of a table or desk. Hoops are very portable and you can embroider nearly anywhere – I even rest the hoop against the steering wheel while waiting in the car for my children! There are hoop stands on the market which hold the hoop away from your lap or the table; however, many of my students find the stands bulky and awkward to work with. Experiment with different ways and decide which one suits you best.*

2. TO PREPARE FOR EMBROIDERY, REFER TO *WHICH THREADS AND COLOURS SHOULD I USE?*, PAGE 10, AND *EMBROIDERY STITCHES*, PAGE 17.

Using embroidery thread

❖ Try to leave one or both wrappers on the skeins to prevent knotting, and remember to refer to the number on the wrapper to make sure that you are using the correct colour (this can be a problem when working at night!).

❖ Never cut a thread longer than from the tip of a finger to 10 cm (4 in) above the elbow (no more than 50 cm (20 in)). It will knot. However, you will have to use a longer thread for couching.

❖ Tie a knot at the cut end.

Using silk ribbon

❖ Silk ribbon 3-4 mm (¹/₈ in) wide may be combined with embroidery thread to enhance some of the designs, adding another dimension to the work.

❖ Use silk ribbon for only some of the stitches, to maintain a balanced design, for example:

– French knots or colonial knots. Wind once around the needle.

– Extended knots. Wind once around the needle.

– Detached chain or larger lazy daisies.

❖ Silk ribbon washes very well and certainly adds character to a design. However, only use it with the stitches suggested above in order to maintain a balanced design.

❖ Keep the ribbon flat and as untwisted as possible while working *(fig. 7)*. Pull the ribbon gently through the different layers as you work so that it does not become tatty.

❖ THREAD THE NEEDLE AS FOLLOWS:

– Insert the thread through the eye of the chenille needle *(fig. 8a)*.

– Push the sharp point of the needle into the short threaded end of the ribbon *(fig. 8b)*.

– Pull the long tail of the ribbon to tighten the 'knot'. By threading the ribbon this way, it cannot be pulled out of the eye of the needle and you will be able to work with very short lengths, thus saving on silk ribbon .

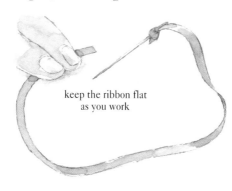

keep the ribbon flat
as you work

FIG. 7

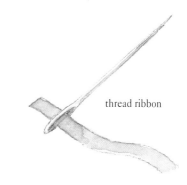

thread ribbon

FIG. 8A

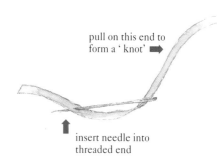

pull on this end to
form a ' knot' ➡

⬆ insert needle into
threaded end

FIG. 8B

HINTS WHEN WORKING
WITH SILK RIBBON

❖ *Cut the ribbon into 30-40 cm (12-15 in) lengths. Too long a ribbon will become tatty and may even tear.*

❖ *Start and end off with a short tail which can be caught in the next stitch. A knot tied in the ribbon is bulky and may loosen in time.*

❖ *Use a no. 22 chenille needle for ribbon work – a needle with a small eye causes the ribbon to fold.*

❖ *When cutting silk ribbon, cut it at an angle so that a sharp point is formed and therefore easier to thread.*

3. BEFORE BEGINNING TO CANDLE-WICK AND QUILT YOUR CHOSEN DESIGN, TAKE NOTE OF THE FOLLOWING:

❖ For a better finish, start with the tightest stitch as follows:

Quilting or running stitch, back stitch, stem stitch, couching, satin stitch, chain stitch, honeycomb, detached chain, lazy daisy, French or colonial knots, lastly adding the beads.

❖ Stitches are made through all three layers of muslin, batting/wadding and fabric, except for a few, such as chain stitch, detached chain, lazy daisies, couching and honeycomb, which are only anchored through all layers.

❖ It does not matter where you start embroidering. Without a hoop you would have to start in the centre of the design and work outwards. The layers, however, cannot move once taut in the hoop and you may start anywhere on the design.

❖ Remember to pull each stitch as tight as possible as you sew. This means that all the stitches will create a quilted look by anchoring the layers together. The only stitches that will not be tightened as you sew are the chain stitch and detached chain.

❖ The stitches suggested are merely guidelines. You may wish to be more creative and make different, more elaborate stitches.

HINTS

❖ *Check the background fabric to see that all the pencil marks are covered before removing the work from the hoop. Fill the flower centres with beads but add French knots in between and along the outer edge of the beads to soften the outline* (fig. 9).

❖ *Hold your embroidery hoop in front of a mirror to get a good idea of what the finished product will look like. Add extra embroidery stitches, beads or silk ribbon until you're satisfied with the design.*

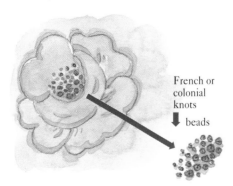

French or colonial knots
↓ beads

FIG. 9

❖ *It is a good idea to sign and date your work, especially a quilt or a framed picture. Lightly trace your name directly on to the picture and use one strand of thread to stem or back stitch the drawn lines. Another idea is to make a name tag on a separate piece of fabric and stitch this label onto the back of your work.*

4. Once the embroidery is complete, remove the work from the hoop.

❖ Complete any corners of the design that were covered by the quilting hoop. Simply pin the corners to the batting/wadding and finish by hand. In many cases it is not necessary to use a hoop. If there is a large section that still needs to be embroidered, use a smaller hoop (for example, a 25 cm (10 in) hoop) and place the corners into the frame as you did before.

❖ Rub the batting/wadding between your fingers to reduce any flattening caused by the hoop.

❖ *See Wiping an article, page 15, if any marks have been made.*

COMBINING CANDLEWICKING WITH FABRIC SHAPES

Combining candlewicking with fabric flowers and leaves adds an interesting dimension to your project and also save hours of work. Fill-in embroidery stitches which are normally required to form the flower or leaf shape are replaced with fabric.

By using fabric shapes, another dimension is added, as well as more colour and definition by embroidering around these shapes (such as the petals, stamens or centres of flowers). These simple shapes are surprisingly easy to make and I encourage beginners to experiment with them.

Use thin fabrics to make these shapes, such as silks, fine cottons or chintz. Do not use upholstery or thick curtaining fabric. Silk works extremely well – once ironed onto the Vilene, it does not fray as badly as cotton fabrics do. The fabric shapes are cut out and glued onto the background with an ordinary glue stick (not liquid glue) and the raw edges of the shapes are candlewicked with French or colonial knots to anchor them to the background fabric. Other embroidery stitches are used to make up the rest of the design.

When making framed articles, it is not necessary to make knots close together as this article will never be washed and the edges will not fray once behind glass. When making washable projects, make two or three rows of knots close together so that the raw edges are completely covered (as you would with a machine appliquéd satin stitch).

Making the fabric shapes

Where I have used fabric shapes in a design, for example, a framed picture (*Still Life* and *Shelley* designs) and on the *Christening Bib*, I have drawn the required shapes on the project page. These are the shapes you will draw onto the shiny side of the iron-on Vilene or fusible webbing.

If you would like to use fabric shapes in one of the larger quarter designs, for a cushion, for example, draw the required shapes from the relevant pattern.

The general rule when combining fabric shapes with embroidery for the larger designs is to choose the biggest flowers for the fabric shapes. The larger leaves are also made in fabric and, as you will not need to fill these flower and leaf shapes with embroidery stitches, the design will be completed in a much shorter period of time.

In the *English Garden* design, for example, draw four corner flowers

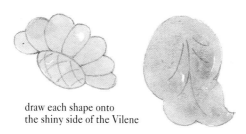

draw each shape onto
the shiny side of the Vilene

FIG 10

onto the Vilene (include all the petal detail) and iron these shapes onto a darker pink fabric. The four flowers in between the corner flowers will also be drawn onto the Vilene and ironed onto a medium-pink fabric. The leaves of the four corner flowers can be ironed onto a medium-green fabric, and the leaves of the four inner flowers can be ironed onto a light-green fabric. The straight, outside squares, the inner circles, the quilt blocks and the petals running from the leaves are all traced onto the design later and will be embroidered with cotton and silk ribbon. It is important to trace each shape *separately*. No overlapping please!

1. Trace the pattern onto tracing paper, make copies and join as described on page 24 (*Make a tracing of the design and join*). You will need this pattern to assemble the project at a later stage.

2. Refer to the project page and note that the leaf, flower and any other relevant shapes have been drawn for you. These shapes will be traced onto Vilene or fusible webbing. Take a strip of iron-on Vilene or webbing, turn it shiny side up and trace the shapes onto it with a soft 3B pencil. Leave a 2 mm (1/16 in) between each shape. Do not allow any shape to touch the adjoining one.

  Trace all the detail as well, for example, the flower centres, petals,

stamens and veins of the leaves *(fig. 10)*. For the *Still Life* vase, draw all the extra detail on the vase.

3. Trace dark lines that will show through later.

4. Cut out each Vilene shape leaving a 3-4 mm (1/8 in) border, following the pencil line as a guide only *(fig. 11)*.

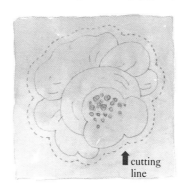

cutting line

FIG. 11

5. Place the Vilene shapes shiny side down onto the wrong side of the chosen fabric.

6. Press with the iron set on the correct temperature. Make sure that the Vilene has bonded well with the fabric and does not lift at the edges.

7. Cut out the Vilene and fabric shapes neatly along the pencil line.

8. Take each shape and place right side up on a glass table or window. Trace all the detail that was previously drawn onto the Vilene with a sharp HB or B pencil onto the right side of fabric. Trace flower centres, petals, dots and veins of leaves. Trace any

other detail as neatly as possible onto the remaining shapes (such as the vase in the *Still Life* design).

HINTS

❖ *When tracing from the larger quarter patterns, remember to add a seam or hem to the shape if it lies underneath another shape, for example, a leaf. This seam will be used to attach the underneath shape to the one above it.*

❖ *Do not cut out on the pencil line. This should only be done once the Vilene is ironed onto the fabric. This prevents the fabric from fraying.*

❖ *I find that Vilene bonds better with the fabric if the iron is not on the steam setting.*

❖ *Only press on the wrong side of the fabric. Do not turn the fabric over and iron on the right side as you may mark it with a dirty iron (the iron may collect glue from the Vilene as you work).*

❖ *If you do happen to turn the Vilene shape shiny side up and the shape adheres to the iron, a hot iron cleaner in a tube or in paste form is available. Use this cleaner to wipe the glue off the hot iron. Use a thick cloth when cleaning.*

❖ *Follow the drawn lines as neatly as possible as you cut out the shape, to ensure a well-assembled project.*

❖ *Use a small, sharp pair of embroidery scissors for precise cutting. It is extremely difficult to cut out small shapes accurately using a large pair of scissors.*

❖ *As the fabric shapes have a nasty habit of getting lost, place them in a saucer or a plastic dish as you work.*

Gluing the fabric shapes
onto the background

1. Pre-wash any cotton background fabric as described on page 23 (*Assembling the project*). It is not necessary to pre-wash synthetic silky fabrics as these do not shrink.

2. Cut out the background fabric as described in step 3 on page 24.

3. Draw the inside square for the cushion and quilt blocks as described in step 3b on page 24. For the smaller projects, refer to the project page for the size of the background block you need.

4. Pin the pattern onto the background fabric as described in step 3c, page 24. Do not trace the design onto the background block at this stage. The fabric shapes will be glued on before tracing.

5. Take the fabric shapes (start with the vase in the *Still Life* design or the leaves with the other designs) and the glue stick. Use a scrap of paper to press on and lightly glue the Vilene side of each shape using the glue stick. Take care to glue the edges so that they do not lift off the background fabric once pressed into place.

6. Take the glued shape and press it onto the background fabric. Press in place using the pinned pattern as a guide for placement. Glue all the shapes onto the background fabric as above *(fig. 12a)*.

7. Do *not* remove the pins and pattern yet. You will first have to trace the remaining detail (which is not covered by the fabric shape) onto the background block.

HINTS

❖ *Use paper scraps to glue on so that you do not end up with a messy table. Discard each scrap after use and start with a fresh page. This prevents the glue from staining the fabric side of the shapes.*

❖ *For most of the cream background fabrics, the design will be visible through the background fabric. If the design is not clear, tape the pattern and fabric to a sunny window or use a glass table with a light underneath it to illuminate the design.*

For very dark fabrics, make a tracing of the pattern and join. Pin the

fabric shapes glued on
FIG. 12A

fabric shapes and detail drawn onto background
FIG. 12B

SILKY FABRICS, THREADS AND BEADS ARE USED TO MAKE UP THE SHELLEY PATTERN

tracing on top of the background fabric and slip the shapes underneath the tracing paper, using the tracing as a guide.

❖ *Where the leaf shape has an extra seam added, the seam or hem will be underneath the flower or adjoining leaf.*

❖ *The Vilene shapes will have changed shape slightly during the ironing and cutting stages, but this will not detract from the overall design. Use the pattern as a guide only. In other words, where a leaf is larger or smaller than indicated on the pattern, you will use embroidery stitches to fill in any gaps.*

Tracing remaining detail onto the background

1. Use an HB or B pencil to trace the remaining details (such as smaller flowers, leaves, stems and so on) onto the background block. Trace all the stems, dots, teardrops, quilting lines and any other detail that is not covered by the fabric shapes. Trace as neatly as possible and use a ruler to draw any straight lines. This detail will be embroidered with cotton or silk thread to complete the design.

2. Remove the pins and the paper pattern.

HINT

Before removing the pins and the pattern, ensure that all the detail has been traced. It is extremely difficult to draw the detail freehand once the layers are in the hoop.

Candlewicking and quilting the design

1. Place the layers into the hoop as described in step 1, page 26. Remember to turn the background block over onto the wrong side and to press the fabric block to remove any creases. The block will never be ironed again once quilted!

2. Prepare for embroidery as described in steps 2 and 3, page 28. Place the layers into the quilting hoop and start embroidering (the embroidery steps are exactly the same regardless of whether or not you have used fabric shapes).

3. START BY ANCHORING THE FABRIC SHAPES AS FOLLOWS:

a. Use two strands of matching embroidery thread and anchor the fabric shapes along the raw edge with French or colonial knots. Anchor the shapes through all the layers of fabric. Start by making a French or colonial knot just on the edge of the fabric shape and proceed along the shape so that the raw edge of the fabric is covered by the knots.

For articles that are going to be framed *(fig. 13a)*, it is not necessary to make the knots that close together – leave a gap of 2 mm (1/16 in). The article will never be washed and cannot fray behind glass. For articles that will be washed (for example, the *Tray Cloth* or *Christening Bib*), the knots must be close together so that the shape will not fray when washed *(fig. 13b)*. Make one, two or even three rows of knots next to each other.

b. Where there are leaves on framed articles, you may prefer to do a quilting or running stitch (instead of French or colonial knots) along the raw edges to save time. Use two strands of embroidery thread and quilt through all the layers to anchor the shape onto the background block.

c. Use a matching colour thread.

4. The fabric shapes can now be embroidered to form the petals, stamens and centres of flowers. The veins of the leaves, too, can be embroidered. Stitch through all the layers using two strands of thread (one strand for very small shapes) and back stitch or stem stitch. Quilting stitch or running stitch may also be used. Stitch along the pencil line through all the layers.

5. Embroider the rest of the design. Refer to page 28 (*Before beginning to candlewick and quilt your design*).

6. Use beads to form the centre of the flower shapes. Fill the gaps between beads with small French knots or colonial knots (use one or two strands of thread). Make knots along the outside curve of the beaded centre to soften the outline of the beads.

7. Add any extra stitches that may be required to fill in any gaps between the fabric shapes. Use French knots or colonial knots with two strands of embroidery thread, or if using silk ribbon, detached chain or extended French knots.

8. Remove the work from the hoop as described in step 4, page 29.

9. For any soiled areas which may have appeared on the fabric block, refer to *Wiping an article*, page 15, and follow these instructions.

Easier than you thought, isn't it?

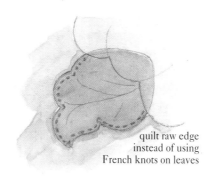

quilt raw edge
instead of using
French knots on leaves

FIG. 13A

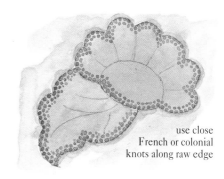

use close
French or colonial
knots along raw edge

FIG. 13B

THE CLIMBING TALISMAN PATTERN USING CANDLEWICKING (LEFT) AND COMBINING CANDLEWICKING WITH FABRIC SHAPES (RIGHT)

FRAMING THE BLOCK

Any reputable framer will be able to advise you on what frame and mounting to choose. You will require two or three mountings placed one on top of the other to make a deep enough recess in which to set the embroidery. Choose two or three different complementary colours for the mountings to enhance the design.

HINTS

❖ *The top mounting (i.e. the mounting that will form the main colour of the framed picture) could be cream, the same colour as the background block. Use a green and a rose colour mounting for the second and third (i.e. the bottommost layer) to form the window of the frame. A square or rectangular mounting is preferable as the oval or round mounts may cause the design to be off-centre if it is not cut accurately, or if the embroidery is slightly off-centre.*

❖ *Ordinary window-pane glass can be used. Non-reflective glass tends to hide the detail of the design.*

❖ *As your work is sure to become a treasured heirloom, it is a good idea to sign and date your work before framing it.*

❖ *It is not necessary to zig-zag or cut off any of the edges. The framer will cut your article to size or he or she will stretch the whole block over a mounting board before framing it.*

HOW TO USE THESE DESIGNS FOR MACHINE APPLIQUÉ

Appliqué means to sew or fix a decoration or trimming of one material onto another. To appliqué by hand, the trimming or shape can be anchored with French knots or colonial knots as described on pages 18 and 19 respectively, or you may like to use satin stitch or buttonhole stitch to cover the raw edges.

To appliqué by machine

The designs in this book are surprisingly versatile and many are suitable for machine appliqué. To appliqué, follow the steps listed under *Combining candlewicking with fabric shapes* on page 29 (*Tracing the remaining detail onto background*). Draw all the shapes you would like to appliqué onto the shiny side of the Vilene.

Instead of fixing the fabric shapes onto the fabric by hand, sew them on by machine using a fine zig-zag or satin stitch. Fix the layers in the quilting hoop and candlewick, embroider or quilt the design as described in *Candlewicking and quilting the design*, page 32.

Please refer to the photographs above for which colours to use in the designs. These photographs also clearly illustrate how the various designs differ when embroidered and when appliquéd.

CUSHIONS AND QUILTS

Making soft furnishings, especially cushions and quilts, is one of the most versatile and economical ways to change your home to reflect your style and personality. A beautiful, hand-made quilt can transform your bedroom, and a pile of pretty, colourful cushions will brighten any dull room or sofa.

PREPARING THE BLOCK FOR A CUSHION OR QUILT

1. Place the quilted block right side down on the ironing board so that the fabric background is face down and the muslin side is showing.
2. Set your iron to the correct temperature. Lift the muslin and batting/wadding so that the wrong side of the fabric block is showing, and test the temperature of the iron on a corner of the wrong side of the fabric *(fig. 1a)* to prevent scorching the fabric.
3. Press the wrong side of the loose fabric block where it has creased in the hoop and at the four corners.
4. Turn the block right side up and pin the background fabric onto the batting/wadding with the pins at right angles to the edge along the drawn pencil line *(fig. 1b)*.
5. Place pins 2.5-3 cm (1 in) apart so that the unpinned fabric will not make a fold as you zig-zag the edge by machine.
6. Use a wide zig-zag stitch that is set so that the stitches are not too far apart, and zig-zag along the drawn pencil line through all the layers. (I sew over the pins but you may wish to remove them as you sew.)
7. Remove the pins and cut along the zig-zag edge to remove the excess fabric, batting/wadding and muslin (keep these for filling cushion pads). If you have cut the zig-zag stitch in error, simply zig-zag over the loose edge again.

HINTS

❖ *When working with silky fabrics, do not allow the iron to rest on any part of the material for longer than a second or two. Rather lift the iron and touch down gently in quick movements. This will prevent scorching. For cotton fabrics, the iron can be moved back and forth without lifting it off the fabric.*

❖ *Do not pin onto the muslin layer as this will cause the fabric to fold between the pins due to the layers being much too thick.*

lift the muslin and batting/ wadding and press wrong side of fabric

FIG. 1A

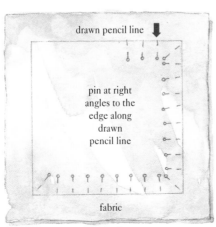

drawn pencil line

pin at right angles to the edge along drawn pencil line

fabric

FIG. 1B

❖ *Pin only through the top fabric and the batting/wadding.*

❖ *As you pin, do not lift the block off the table. Rather smooth the fabric section you are pinning from the centre out with your free hand, as you would when ironing. Pin as you 'iron' the creases by hand, slipping the pin into the batting/wadding without lifting the block off the table. This results in a flat, smooth edge, free of puckers.*

FINISHING A CUSHION

There are several ways to finish a cushion. Finish cushions for the bedroom with a frill or use lace in a complementary colour. Cushion cord and binding are effective when used to finish more elegant cushions for the lounge or study, for example. The six cushions here were made using the *Ambience*, *Balmoral*, *Fantasy*, *Constantia*, *Serenade* and *Sarah* designs.

FINISHING A CUSHION WITH LACE

Materials required

The measurements given below are for a 42 x 42 cm (16½ x 16½ in) cushion block. Please adjust your measurements accordingly if making a different size cushion.

1. 4 m x 3-5 cm (4 yds x 1½-2 in) lace to complement the colour of the fabric block. Use fine synthetic lace for silky fabrics and cotton lace for calico and glazed cotton (chintz).

2. 50-60 cm (about ¹/₂ yd) good quality cream, complementary or matching fabric for the backing slips.

3. 50-60 cm (about ¹/₂ yd) inexpensive fabric for the cushion pad which will be stuffed.

4. One bag of polyester toy filling, down or feather filling, or wool fibres with which to stuff the cushion pad. Foam chips are not recommended as these can become hard and lumpy after a while.

5. EQUIPMENT
– steam iron with a protective cover;
– sewing machine and threads;
– ruler or tape measure;
– sharp pair of fabric scissors;
– dressmakers' pins; and
– needle and thread.

HINTS

❖ *Polyester filling is a must for those allergic to feathers or wool.*

❖ *Remember to pre-wash all cotton fabrics to allow for shrinkage and to remove excess printing dyes.*

How to finish a
lace-edged cushion

1. PIN THE LACE TO THE PREPARED BLOCK *See Preparing the block for a cushion or quilt*, page 35.

a. Lay the lace along the zigzagged edge of the block. With right sides facing, pin the lace and fabric block together.

b. It is not necessary to gather the lace. An easier method is to pin small (4 mm (¹/₈ in)) pleats or folds into the lace as you work which should be about 2.5-3 cm (1-1¹/₂ in) apart.

c. The pins must be placed at right angles to the edge of the cushion so that you can sew over them – this way you will not have to tack the lace onto the block.

d. Make extra pleats or folds at each corner so that a rounded edge is

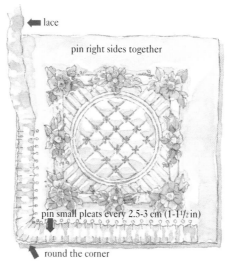

FIG. 2

formed. This allows the lace to lie open once the cushion is complete *(fig. 2)*. Ensure that the pleats or folds do not lie near the edge to be stitched later as the lace will then be sewn into the seam and spoil the finish.

e. To finish, overlap the lace at the starting point by 3-4 cm (1¹/₂-1³/₄ in). It is not necessary to make a fold or pleat in this overlap as it will be underneath the starting point. Cut off the excess lace.

f. Do not remove the pins until the backing slips have been sewn on.

2. MAKE THE BACKING SLIPS

a. You will need two pieces of backing fabric, 50 x 42 cm (20 x 16¹/₂ in). Always cut the backing slips larger than the block to allow for the stretching of the batting/wadding as you sew. Cut down to size later.

b. The width of the slips will be about three-quarters the size of the block to allow for a large overlap.

c. On both pieces of fabric, make a 2 cm (1 in) fold along one of the 50 cm (20 in) lengths. Press in place. Fold over 2 cm (1 in) again and press.

d. Machine stitch along folded hems.

3. SEW THE BACKING SLIPS ON

a. Take one piece of backing and, with right sides together, pin onto the

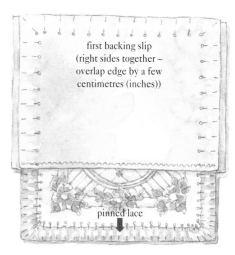

FIG. 3A

cushion block. The backing slip should overlap the zig-zagged edges by a few centimetres (about ¹/₂ in) to allow for any stretching that may take place as you sew *(fig. 3a)*.

b. The backing slip should be pinned over the lace pins, with the pins at right angles to the edge.

c. Take the second piece of backing and, with right sides together, pin to the remaining edge of the fabric block. Leave an overlap of 15 cm (6 in) to prevent the slips from gaping when filled *(fig. 3b)*.

d. Turn the block over, muslin-side up. Straight stitch through all the

FIG. 3B

layers, using the inner edge of the zig-zag stitch as a guide and leaving a 6 mm (1/4 in) seam. Sew over the pins or tacking thread.

e. Turn the block gently as you sew to make rounded corners.

f. Remove the pins from the backing slips. Place your hand inside the cover and remove all the pins from the lace.

g. Cut off the excess backing fabric, cutting off the points at the corners. You may wish to zig-zag the raw edges through all the layers but I never normally do this for cushions.

h. Do not turn the cushion cover right side out at this stage. The bag must first be measured and cut, using the cushion cover as a guide.

4. MAKE THE CUSHION BAG

a. Take your inexpensive piece of fabric for the pad and fold it in half. Pin the two pieces together so that the fabric cannot move.

b. Place the inside-out cushion cover on top of the pad fabric and, using a ruler and pencil, draw the outline of the cushion cover onto the pad fabric.

c. Straight stitch the two layers of the fabric pad together along the drawn line, leaving a 25 cm (10 in) gap along one edge *(fig. 4)*.

THIS CHARMING CUSHION (SPRAYMIST PATTERN) IS FINISHED WITH A FABRIC FRILL

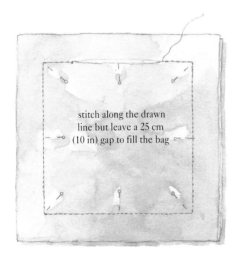

stitch along the drawn line but leave a 25 cm (10 in) gap to fill the bag

FIG. 4

5. FILLING THE CUSHION PAD

I use polyester toy filling for most of my cushions as it is an inexpensive filling. Although pricey, feathers or down are still the best option as these fibres help the cushion retain its shape; they are also heavier than polyester and the cushion will therefore not fall off the sofa easily.

a. Turn the pad right side out and use a pair of scissors to push the corners out neatly.

b. Make balls of filling and stuff the four corners first.

c. Now stuff the edges along three of the sides so that firm, well-filled edges are formed.

d. Fill the centre of the pad to make a nice, fat cushion.

e. Lastly, fill the open edge so that the filling bulges slightly out of the pad.

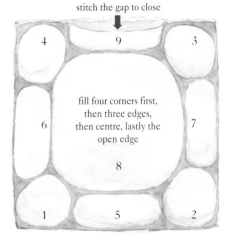

stitch the gap to close

fill four corners first, then three edges, then centre, lastly the open edge

FIG. 5

f. Pin the gap together and hem stitch or whip stitch closed *(fig. 5)*.

6. PLACE THE PAD INSIDE THE CUSHION COVER

a. Insert the pad in the cushion cover between the two backing slips.

b. Push the four corners of the pad neatly into the corners of the cover.

c. Shake and pat the cover until the filling is evenly spread throughout.

d. If you like, hem stitch along the folded hem of the backing slip to close it and form a neat back. These stitches can be cut when removing the pad to wash the cushion cover.

HINTS

❖ *Use a commerical starch spray when pressing. See Handy Hints, number 12 on page 14.*

❖ *To make a more interesting hem, use a fancy stitch instead of a straight one.*

❖ *Pin the top backing slip along the hemmed edge to prevent the slip from folding back when stitching the layers together.*

❖ *Make sure that all the pins are removed or they will damage your scissors when cutting the backing fabric to size.*

❖ *I sew over the lace and backing pins. If you do not wish to do this, first tack on the lace before attaching the backing slips, then tack the backing slips to the fabric block.*

❖ *Do not cut off the excess fabric of the pad. This fabric will make neater corners and edges once the bag is turned inside out.*

FINISHING A CUSHION WITH A FABRIC FRILL

Materials required

See Finishing a cushion with lace, page 35 and, instead of the lace, use 80 cm (80 in) of fabric for the frill in a colour to match the cushion block.

Refer to the section *Preparing the block for a cushion or quilt*, page 35. A double frill ensures that there is no hem on the underside of the frill, giving a better finish.

How to finish a cushion with a fabric frill

A good size frill to cut is 15-20 cm (6-8 in) x 4 m (4¼ yds).

1. Join three or four strips to make a 4 m (4¼ yds) long frill, open the seams and press flat.

2. Join the strips along the two short edges to make a circle *(fig. 6a)*. Open the seams and press flat.

join frill at two short, raw edges to make a circle

15-20 cm (6-8 in) wide

4 m (4¼ yds) long

FIG. 6A

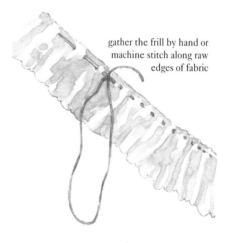

gather the frill by hand or machine stitch along raw edges of fabric

FIG. 6B

3. Fold the frill in half, wrong sides together, and press along the folded edge. Use a commercial starch spray (*see Handy Hints*, number 12, page 14) when ironing. This helps to keep the fabric flat.

4. Divide the frill into quarters by folding the frill in half and in half again. Insert a pin at each quarter. Pin at right angles to the edge. These quarter marks will guide you when you are pinning the frill onto the cushion block.

5. Gather the frill by hand or machine stitch along the raw edges of the fabric *(fig. 6b)*. This circle of fabric must fit the cushion block so that the quarter mark pins are placed at each corner and the corners rounded. Gather the frill so that there are extra folds at each corner – this will ensure that the frill will fold out neatly once you have completed the cushion.

6. With right sides together, pin the frill onto the fabric edge as you would for the lace finish (*see* step 1, page 36) with the pins at right angles to the edge *(fig. 6c)*.

7. Stitch the frill onto the cushion as for the lace-edged cushion described on page 36.

8. MAKE THE BACKING SLIPS
See step 2, page 36.

9. SEW THE BACKING SLIPS ON
See step 3, page 36.

10. MAKE THE CUSHION PAD
See step 4, page 37.

11. FILLING THE CUSHION PAD
See step 5, page 37.

12. PLACE THE PAD INSIDE THE CUSHION COVER
See step 6, page 37.

HINT

Pin lace along the raw edge of the folded frill after step 3. Pin at right angles to the edge. Proceed with step 4.

pin the frill to the cushion block

FIG. 6C

ADD A STYLISH TOUCH TO A CUSHION BY FINISHING IT OFF WITH CORD AND A TASSEL

FINISHING THE CUSHION WITH CORD

Cushion cord is available from upholstery and curtaining stores and is purchased by the metre (yard). Choose a complementary colour to the cushion fabric. It is a good idea to pre-wash cushion cord in tepid water to allow for shrinkage and to remove any excess dye. Do not use hot water as the heat may damage the cord.

Materials required

See Finishing a cushion with lace, page 35 and instead of the lace, use 2 m (2 yds) of cushion cord.

How to finish a cushion with cord

Refer to the section *Preparing the block for a cushion or quilt*, page 35 – the block will be prepared in exactly the same way.

1. MAKE THE BACKING SLIPS
See step 2, page 36.

2. SEW THE BACKING SLIPS ON
See step 3, page 36.

3. MAKE THE CUSHION PAD
See step 4, page 37.

4. FILLING THE CUSHION PAD
See step 5, page 37.

5. PLACE THE PAD INSIDE THE CUSHION COVER
It is much easier to sew the cord on once the cushion is filled so that the fabric does not pucker during sewing. *See* step 6, page 37.

6. ATTACH THE CUSHION CORD
   a. Take the filled cushion cover and carefully snip the stitching at one of the corners to make an opening of approximately 2.5-3 cm (1-1¹/₂ in).

The ends of the cord will be inserted into this opening.

   b. Use approximately 2 m (2 yds) of cord per cushion. Whip stitch the one raw end of the cord to prevent it from unravelling.

   c. Insert about 4-5 cm (2 in) of the sewn end of the cord into the opening. Pin in place. Wind the cord around the filled cushion along the sewn seam, pinning it in place as you go.

   d. When you reach the starting point, cut off the excess cord, leaving a tail of 4-5 cm (2 in).

   e. Whip stitch the loose tail of the cord as before to prevent it from unravelling.

   f. Insert this end in the opening so that a rounded corner is formed, exactly the same as the other three corners. Pin in place.

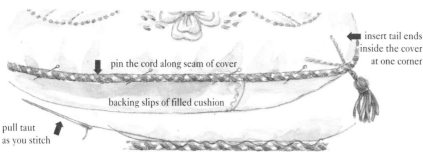

pin the cord along seam of cover

insert tail ends
inside the cover
at one corner

backing slips of filled cushion

pull taut
as you stitch

FIG. 7

g. Stitch the cord in place using an embroidery needle and two strands of matching embroidery thread, as follows *(fig. 7):*

– Begin by knotting the thread. Insert the needle in the batting/wadding part of the cushion cover above the cushion seam.

– Catch a section of the cord and re-insert the needle in the cushion cover. Pull the thread taut so that the stitch does not show.

– Use a tiny hem stitch *(see page 42)* (or any stitch you choose) in a matching thread to close the open corner of the cushion cover. Pull the stitches taut so that the back and the front of the cushion meet.

HINTS

❖ *Catch the fabric and batting/wadding section of the front part of the cushion cover and not the backing slips. This way the thread will be inserted in the thicker*

front of the cushion cover and the inside pad will not be sewn down in error. The cushion pad will need to be removed when washing the cushion cover.

❖ *If you would like to add a tassel to a corner of the cushion, choose a cushion tassel or a small key tassel in a shade that matches the cord. To attach it, remove one end of the pinned cord before stitching this end onto the cushion. Slip stitch the tassel onto the cord. Re-insert the cord in the opening and stitch the cord in place.*

FINISHING THE CUSHION WITH BINDING

Using binding to finish a cushion is much easier than using piping. The cushion block and backing slips are sewn with wrong sides together, after which the binding is attached. Use a contrasting colour for the binding that will complement the cushion.

Before starting, refer to the section *Preparing the block for a cushion or quilt block*, page 35.

Materials required

See Finishing a cushion with lace, page 35 but instead of lace, use 15 cm (6 in) of fabric for binding.

1. MAKING THE BINDING

Bias binding is available ready-made but the idea here is to use a hand-made binding in a contrasting colour to complement the fabric you are using for the cushion cover. Use silky or cotton fabrics.

a. Decide how wide you would like the folded binding to be. I normally make mine 4 cm (1½ in) wide but you may prefer something wider. It is not advisable to make binding less than 4 cm (1½ in) wide as it becomes extremely difficult to fold it over the different layers. Draw two strips along the entire width of the fabric (usually 115 cm (45 in)).

BINDING IS ANOTHER EFFECTIVE METHOD OF FINISHING OFF A CUSHION

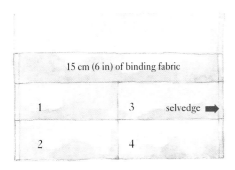

15 cm (6 in) of binding fabric

| 1 | 3 | selvedge ➡ |
| 2 | 4 | |

FIG. 8A

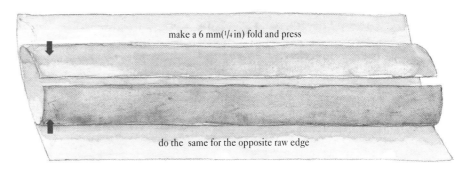

make a 6 mm (¼ in) fold and press

do the same for the opposite raw edge

FIG. 8B

b. Divide these two strips in half so that four strips are drawn, each 57 cm (22½ in) in length *(fig. 8a)*.

c. Cut along the drawn lines.

d. Spray the fabric with a commercial starch spray *(see Handy Hints number 12, page 14)* and use an iron set on the correct temperature.

e. Make a 6 mm (¼ in) fold, wrong sides facing, along the length of one of the edges of the fabric and press in place. Do the same for the opposite raw edge *(fig. 8b)*. All four strips are folded and pressed in this way.

f. Fold the fabric strips in half again and press in place. The 4 cm (1½ in) strip is now about 1.5 cm (½ in) wide.

2. MAKE THE BACKING SLIPS
See step 2, page 36.

3. SEW THE BACKING SLIPS ON
This is the only method where the backing slips are sewn on with wrong sides together (i.e. the cushion is not stitched and then turned right side out).

a. Take one backing slip and pin it onto the muslin side of the cushion block, wrong sides together. Allow the backing slip to overlap the zig-zagged edges by a few centimetres (about ½ in) to allow for any stretching that may occur as you sew.

b. Pin with the pins at right angles to the edge *(fig. 9a)*.

c. Take the second backing slip and pin it along the remaining edges of the muslin block. Allow for an overlap of 15 cm (6 in) to prevent the slips from gaping when filled *(fig. 9b)*.

d. Turn the cushion block over so that the right (fabric) side is facing up. Use the inner edge of the zig-zag stitch as a guide, leaving a 6 mm (¼ in) seam. Straight stitch through all the layers, sewing over the pins or the tacking thread.

e. Do not make rounded corners. Follow the square shape of the block.

f. Remove all the pins from the backing slips.

g. Cut off the excess backing fabric, leaving the corners square.

h. Zig-zag the raw edges through all the layers to form neat, flat edges along all four sides.

4. MAKE THE CUSHION PAD
See step 4, page 37.

first backing slip

muslin side of block

FIG. 9A

pin second backing slip along remaining edges of muslin block

FIG. 9B

5. ATTACH THE BINDING STRIPS
Each binding strip is attached separately at different stages.

a. Pin the first strip of binding, right sides together, onto the front (right side) of the cushion cover, with pins at right angles to the edge. Cut off excess binding fabric. Stitch through all the layers along the first pressed fold, sewing over the pins *(fig. 10a)*.

FIG. 10A

b. Pin the second strip of binding as for point 5a (above) and stitch through all the layers *(fig. 10b)*.

FIG. 10B

c. Remove the pins.

d. Open the two attached binding strips fully to lie right side up along the edge of the cushion.

FIG. 10C

e. Attach the third strip from the raw edge of the opened binding (1) to the opened raw edge of the opened binding (2). Stitch through all layers along the first pressed fold of the binding. Cut off excess binding fabric *(fig. 10c)*.

f. Do the same as described above for the fourth strip *(fig. 10d)*.

FIG. 10D

g. Remove all the pins.

h. Fold the first two binding strips to the back of the cushion. Turn in the first pressed fold and fold in half along the centre to form a neat edge from one raw edge to the next.

i. Fold the third and fourth strips over, folding the raw edges of strips one and two at the same time to make neat, square corners *(fig. 10e)*.

FIG. 10E

6. STITCH THE BINDING TO THE BACK OF THE CUSHION

The binding is sewn to the back of the cushion cover by hand. Machine stitching would show on the front of the cover. Use a matching thread and a blind hem stitch *(see fig. 11b below)* to sew along the folded edge of the binding. Use an overcasting stitch to neaten the four folded corners.

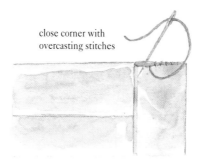

close corner with overcasting stitches

FIG. 11A

a. Start by knotting the thread and inserting the needle through the open corner. Use tiny overcasting stitches to close the corner. Remember not to pull too tightly, otherwise the fabric will pucker *(fig. 11a)*.

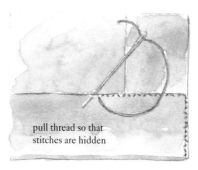

pull thread so that stitches are hidden

FIG. 11B

Proceed down the folded binding using a blind hem stitch. This stitch is sewn on the inside fold of the hem, thereby making the stitch almost invisible *(fig. 11b)*.

Hold the cushion cover so that the folded hem is facing you. Make a small stitch *inside* the folded edge of the hem. Catch a thread of the backing fabric on the point of the needle

before making another stitch inside the folded edge of the hem.

b. End off with three or four small back stitches. Pull the thread taut.

7. FILLING THE CUSHION PAD

See step 5, page 37.

8. PLACE THE PAD INSIDE THE CUSHION COVER

See step 6, page 37.

HINTS

❖ *It is not necessary to cut the binding on the bias of the fabric as no rounded corners are made when attaching the binding.*

❖ *Pin the top backing slip along the hemmed edge to prevent the slip from folding back when stitching the layers together.*

❖ *I sew over the pins when stitching the layers together. If you do not want to do this, then tack the backing slips to the cushion block instead.*

CALCULATING THE NUMBER OF BLOCKS FOR A QUILT

This information applies to a quilt without sashing (borders). Sashing is extra work and not essential for these designs. Cord or lace added after the quilt blocks have been joined have the same function as sashing but are easier to apply.

❖ Most of the silky fabrics are 115 cm (45 in) wide. You will be able to get roughly four blocks per 1.25 m (1^1/$_4$ yds).

❖ Cut *all* the quilt blocks 57 x 57 cm (22^1/$_2$ x 22^1/$_2$ in) square so that each square will fit snugly into the 45.7 cm (18 in) hoop. This ensures that the design to be embroidered will be inside the hoop and therefore you will not have to move the hoop to embroider the rest of the design. On this larger fabric square draw another block, the size of which is calculated according to the size of your mattress.

BEAUTIFUL SOFT FURNISHINGS REFLECT YOUR STYLE AND PERSONALITY

❖ *See Which fabrics and colours should I choose*, page 9 and *How much fabric should I purchase?*, page 9.

❖ Inside each 57 x 57 cm (22^1/2 x 22^1/2 in) block draw the following size square:

a. For a single, twin, double or standard king-size mattress, draw a 50 x 50 cm (20 x 20 in) square.

b. For a queen-size or extra-long king-size mattress, draw a 55 x 55 cm (21^1/2 x 21^1/2 in) square.

– This inside square will only be edged and cut down to size once all the embroidery is complete.

– Use an HB or B pencil to draw the lines onto the fabric and a T-square to make a perfect square.

Estimate how many blocks you will need for your quilt according to *fig. 12* below. Please check your mattress size and determine the measurements accordingly. As the blocks are square, you will need to adjust the measurements according to your desired quilt size so that it will fit the length and width of the mattress.

HINTS

❖ *Use a cardboard template for quilt-making as each block needs to be exactly the same size.* See Handy Hints number 3, page 14.

❖ *Always purchase an extra metre (yard) or two of fabric when planning a quilt in case of mistakes. Also, the dye lots of fabric may differ if you buy extra fabric at a later date. Extra fabric will never go to waste – it can always be used to make cushions, curtain tie-backs or a table cloth.*

❖ *Strips of fabric and batting/wadding can be added to the sides of the quilt for the overhang. These strips are joined onto the embroidered blocks and are quilted along the length of the fabric. This saves the time and expense of making two extra rows of blocks to make up the quilt.*

How much fabric do I need?

❖ Calculate four blocks per 1.25 m (1^1/4 yds) (*see How much fabric do I purchase?*, page 9).

❖ Estimate an extra 6 m (6^1/2 yds) for the sides (overhang) of the quilt and the binding.

See fig. 13 for a breakdown of the 6 m (6^1/2 yds) to be used for the overhang of the quilt.

❖ If you'd like the quilt to hang right onto the floor and your bed is higher than 45 cm (19 in) (measured from the edge of the joined quilted blocks to the floor), you will need to buy an extra 3 m (3^1/4 yds) of fabric to make the binding strips. For a height less than 45 cm (19 in), the binding fabric will be cut from the 6 m (6^1/2 yds) purchased for the overhang, as indicated by the darkened areas in *fig. 13*.

❖ You will need more or less the same meterage (yardage) for the batting/ wadding and muslin. Adjust the amount required according to the width of the batting/wadding and muslin if they are greater or less than 115 cm (45 in) wide.

JOINING THE QUILT

Joining the blocks

Refer to *Preparing the block for a cushion or quilt*, page 35. Each block will be prepared according to these instructions before they are joined. It

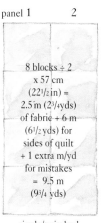

panel 1   2

8 blocks ÷ 2 x 57 cm (22^1/2 in) = 2.5 m (2^3/4 yds) of fabric + 6 m (6^1/2 yds) for sides of quilt + 1 extra m/yd for mistakes = 9.5 m (9^3/4 yds)

single/twin bed

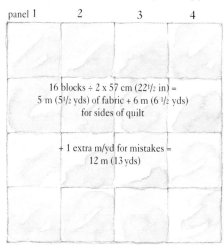

panel 1   2   3   4

16 blocks ÷ 2 x 57 cm (22^1/2 in) = 5 m (5^1/2 yds) of fabric + 6 m (6^1/2 yds) for sides of quilt

+ 1 extra m/yd for mistakes = 12 m (13 yds)

king-size bed

panel 1   2   3

12 blocks ÷ 2 x 57 cm (22^1/2 in) = 3.5 m (3^3/4 yds) of fabric + 6 m (6^1/2 yds) for sides of quilt

+ 1 extra m/yd for mistakes = 10.5 m (10^3/4 yds)

double bed

panel 1   2   3

12 blocks ÷ 2 x 57 cm (22^1/2 in) = 3.5 m (3^3/4 yds) of fabric + 6 m (6^1/2 yds) for sides of quilt

+ 1 extra m/yd for mistakes = 10.5 m (10^3/4 yds)

queen-size bed

FIG. 12

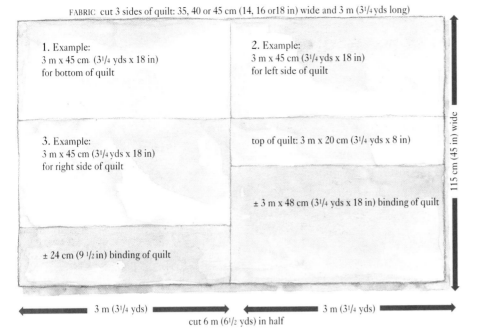

FABRIC cut 3 sides of quilt: 35, 40 or 45 cm (14, 16 or18 in) wide and 3 m (3¼ yds long)

1. Example:
3 m x 45 cm (3¼ yds x 18 in)
for bottom of quilt

2. Example:
3 m x 45 cm (3¼ yds x 18 in)
for left side of quilt

3. Example:
3 m x 45 cm (3¼ yds x 18 in)
for right side of quilt

top of quilt: 3 m x 20 cm (3¼ yds x 8 in)

± 3 m x 48 cm (3¼ yds x 18 in) binding of quilt

± 24 cm (9 ½ in) binding of quilt

115 cm (45 in) wide

3 m (3¼ yds)

3 m (3¼ yds)

cut 6 m (6½ yds) in half

FIG. 13 DIVIDING THE FABRIC

3. With rights sides together, machine stitch through all six layers, leaving a 1 cm (³/₈ in) seam. Sew the panels together in this way to form two, three or four panels, depending on the size of the quilt. Remove the pins.

4. Lay the joined panels on a table or on the floor, right side up. Make sure that the panels are lying as you arranged them. It is very easy to inadvertently turn the panel so that it is lying with the bottom block at the top, with the result that some designs are upside down when joined.

HINTS

❖ *Always open out the joined blocks next to the unjoined ones before pinning, to ensure that the design is not upside down.*

is very important, however, to make the blocks exactly the same size so that, when joined, the seams will be perfectly aligned.

❖ The blocks are first joined together to form a row or panel. The rows or panels are joined to make up the quilt, as described below. These rows will lie on top of the mattress. The sides of the quilt will be sewn on later (*see* page 46).

1. Lay the blocks on a large table or on the floor and arrange your design, remembering that the corners and the middle of the quilt are the most important. Lay out the blocks in two, three or four panels of four squares, depending on the size of the quilt.

2. With right sides together, pin one block to the other, with the pins at right angles to the edge of the blocks and 3-4 cm (1-2 in) apart. You will sew over the pins later. Pin the adjoining block to the two joined blocks and proceed to join the whole row of blocks to make a panel. Match up the corners of the blocks first, then ease in the centre to make it fit.

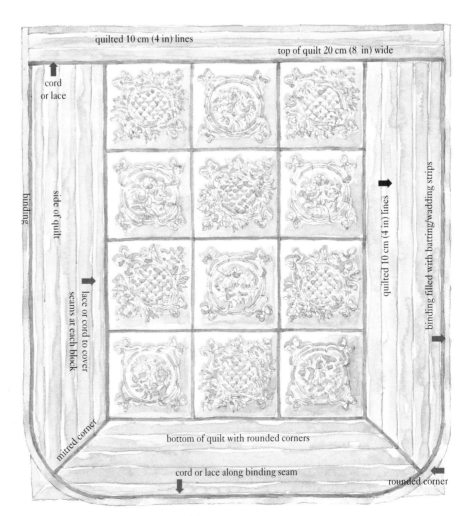

quilted 10 cm (4 in) lines

top of quilt 20 cm (8 in) wide

cord or lace

binding

side of quilt

lace or cord to cover seams at each block

mitred corner

quilted 10 cm (4 in) lines

binding filled with batting/wadding strips

bottom of quilt with rounded corners

cord or lace along binding seam

rounded corner

FIG. 14 JOINING THE BLOCKS

❖ *Arrange your blocks so that the round designs are in the centre row, for example, and the square designs at the corners of the quilt. The four oval designs could form the sides of the quilt. Another option is to lay the busiest patterns to form the centre and corners of the quilt. The quilt must be balanced – too many heavy designs on one side will result in an uneven look.*

Sewing on the sides of the quilt

❖ The length of the fabric for the sides of the quilt is always 3 m (3¹/₄ yds). Excess fabric is cut off later. Divide the 6 m (6¹/₂ yds) you have purchased in two (*see How much fabric do I need*, page 44) so that there are 2 x 3 m (3¹/₄ yds) lengths. Each 3 m (3¹/₄ yds) length is then cut up into the widths you require for the sides and binding of the quilt. (*See fig. 12*, page 44, *How much fabric do I need?*.) This diagram will show you how each 3 m (3¹/₄ yds) length is cut up for the quilt.

❖ The width of the fabric for the sides of the quilt depends on how far you would like the quilt to hang from the floor. Measure the distance from the top of the mattress or the edge of the quilted and joined blocks on the bed, to the required drop. Add on 2 cm (1 in) for seams. (For example, you may like the width to be 35-40 cm (14-16 in) if you have a nightfrill/valance on your bed. A 45 cm (18 in) drop would cover the nightfrill.)

❖ Three strips of fabric are required for the two sides and bottom of the quilt. Each strip is 3 m (3¹/₄ yds) in length. The width depends on the drops you've measured.

❖ One strip of fabric, 3 m (3¹/₄ yds) in length, is required for the top part of the quilt. The width of the strip should be 20 cm (8 in). This strip will be cut from the fabric left over from the second 3 m (3¹/₄ yds) length.

❖ Quilting the sides of the quilt 'shrinks' the fabric, making the sides shorter than measured. It is not necessary to add on more than 2 cm (1 in) seams, however, as the binding finish makes up for the shortfall. The binding added is wide, padded and serves as a 'frame'.

❖ Take the prepared lengths of fabric strips and draw the quilting lines onto the right side of the fabric along the length of the strips. Draw light pencil lines 10 cm (4 in) apart. These lines will be quilted after the strips are added onto the blocks.

❖ Attach the strips for the sides of the quilt to the blocks as described below:

1. ADD THE BOTTOM STRIP TO THE QUILT BLOCKS

a. Take the 3 m (3¹/₄ yds) strip for the bottom of the quilt and, with right sides together, lay the fabric on top of the joined blocks. Allow the excess length to hang equally over the left and right hand sides of the quilt, for example, 50 cm or 1 m (20 in or 1 yd), depending on the size of the quilt you are making (*fig. 15a*).

b. Pin the fabric strip onto the zig-zagged edge of the blocks, pinning at right angles to the edge.

c. Machine stitch through all the layers following the pins, leaving a

1 cm (³/₈ in) seam. Start on the edge of the first block and end on the edge of the last block (i.e. stitch only where the fabric is pinned).

d. Remove the pins and open the fabric to lie flat.

e. Do not cut away any excess fabric at this stage.

2. JOIN THE LEFT SIDE STRIP TO THE QUILTED BLOCKS

a. Take the left side strip and, with right sides together, pin on top of the joined blocks as above. Pin at right angles to the edge and so that the side strip starts at the zig-zagged edge of the top block of the quilt and ends just beyond the bottom strip of fabric (*fig. 15b*). The extra strip of fabric along the bottom of the quilt will be needed later to mitre the corners.

b. It is important to only pin the fabric along the joined blocks. Do not

FIG. 15B

pin along the edge of the fabric strip at the bottom. Leave the top strip lying loose on top of the bottom fabric strip.

c. Machine stitch through all the layers as before, leaving a 1 cm (³/₈ in) seam. Stitch only from the first pin to the last (i.e. only stitch the fabric to the joined blocks).

d. Remove all the pins.

e. Do not cut the fabric at this stage.

3. JOIN THE RIGHT SIDE STRIP TO THE QUILT BLOCKS

drawn quilting lines

join here

◄ 50 cm-1 m
(20 in-1yd) longer

bottom strip of fabric

FIG. 15A

FIG. 15C

a. Take the right side strip and, with right sides together, pin on top of the joined blocks as before. Remember to leave the fabric lying over the bottom strip free of pins *(fig. 15c)*.

b. Stitch from pin to pin, as above.

c. Remove all the pins.

d. Do not cut the fabric at this stage.

4. JOIN THE TOP STRIP TO THE QUILT BLOCKS

a. The top strip is added last as it is sewn from the raw edge of the left fabric strip and along the joined quilted blocks to the raw edge of the right fabric strip. The strip is thus sewn along the fabric and along the joined blocks *(fig. 15d)*.

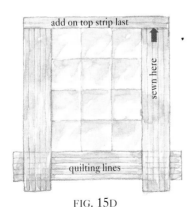

FIG. 15D

b. Take the top strip and, with right sides together, pin on top of the joined blocks as before. Place so that the top strip slants at the raw edge and ends or overlaps the edge of the opposite side strip. These corners will not be mitred

STRIPS OF QUILTED FABRIC ARE ADDED TO FORM THE BORDERS OF THE QUILT

and the edges are not left free. Pin from raw edge to raw edge.

c. Stitch from pin to pin, leaving a 1 cm (³/₈ in) seam as before.

d. Remove all the pins.

e. Cut off the excess fabric along the edge of the top strip so that a neat corner is formed.

5. ATTACHING THE BATTING/ WADDING STRIPS

The fabric strips must be folded back and pinned out of the way onto the quilt blocks. Pin so that the fabric lies

neatly at the edge of the blocks without creasing *(fig. 16)*.

❖ Cut batting/wadding strips 5 cm (2 in) wider and longer than the fabric strips to allow for 'shrinkage' when quilting along the pencil lines. For example, for a 45 cm (18 in) strip, the batting/wadding will be 50 cm (20 in).

❖ Lay batting/wadding on top of the rows of blocks and, as for the fabric strips, pin and sew along the edge of the blocks through all five layers, as follows:

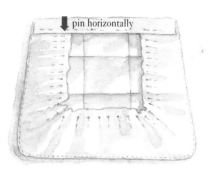

FIG. 16

a. Sew the bottom strip of batting/wadding on first, leaving the sides of the batting/wadding strip (as for the fabric strips) free for mitring.

b. Sew the two sides of batting/wadding on as for the fabric strip, leaving the bottom edges free.

c. Sew the top strip of batting/wadding on last.

d. Remove all the pins from the batting/wadding.

HINTS

❖ *The right side of the batting/wadding is the soft, fluffy side.*

❖ *Carefully check that all the pins have been removed. It is easy to leave an unwanted guest behind in the batting/wadding!*

6. ATTACHING THE MUSLIN STRIPS

The batting/wadding must now be pinned neatly away on top of the folded fabric strips and the rows of joined blocks.

❖ Muslin strips are cut exactly the same size as the batting/wadding.

❖ Lay the muslin on top of the batting/wadding, fabric and blocks as you did for the fabric strips. Machine stitch through all six layers as follows:

a. Sew the bottom strip on first, leaving the sides of the muslin strip free for mitring.

b. Sew on the two sides as for fabric strips, leaving the bottom edges free.

c. Sew on the top strip of muslin last.

d. Remove all the pins from the quilt.

Mitre the corners

❖ Only the bottom corners of the quilt are mitred, as follows:

1. Allow the three layers of fabric, batting/wadding and muslin to fall over the sides of a table, or open out the quilt on the floor.

FIG. 17

2. Fold the top fabric strips out of the way, as before, so that the batting/wadding is exposed *(fig. 17)*. Fold the muslin to the back of the quilt and pin neatly out of the way, as you did for the fabric strips.

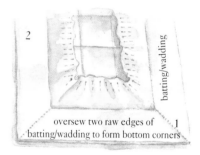

FIG. 18

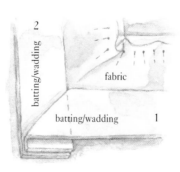

FIG. 19

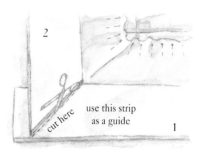

FIG. 20

3. Mitre the batting/wadding at the two bottom corners. Lay the bottom and side strips on top of each other (it does not matter which one is on top). For example, lay the bottom strip of batting/wadding *(no. 1 in fig. 17)* on top of the side strip of batting/wadding (no. 2).

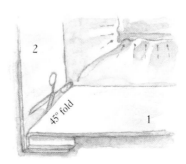

FIG. 21

4. Fold the top strip *(no. 1 in fig. 18)* so that a 45 degree corner is formed. (Fold the batting/wadding backwards so that the right sides are facing.)

5. Cut the no. 2 strip *(fig. 19)*, using the no. 1 folded strip as a guide.

6. Unfold the no. 1 strip and lay the no. 2 (mitred) strip on top of this one.

FIG. 22

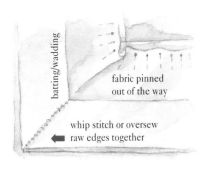

FIG. 23

Cut the no. 1 top strip, using the no. 2 strip as a guide *(fig. 20)*.

7. Oversew the two raw edges of batting/wadding together using large, loose whip stitches. You may like to 'dovetail' the batting in place by cutting steps *(fig. 21)* into the raw edges of the batting/wadding. Whip stitch or oversew in place at the top and the bottom using loose stitches so that the batting/wadding does not pucker *(fig. 22)*.

8. Do the same for the opposite bottom corner of the quilt *(fig. 23)*. Be careful of stray pins – batting/wadding collects pins easily.

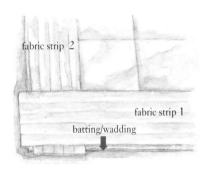

FIG. 24

9. Remove the pins from the fabric strips and unfold to lie flat on top of the batting/wadding *(fig. 24)*. Do not remove the pins from the muslin at the back of the quilt yet. Fold a 45 degree corner on the fabric (as for the batting/wadding). Make sure that the quilted pencil lines are lined up at the corners so that there is a perfect join.

10. Fold the top (no. 1) fabric strip over backwards (i.e. with right sides together) to lie on top of strip no. 2 until the corner is mitred and a neat edge is formed. There is no need to fold or cut the no. 2 strip. Allow this strip to lie straight (i.e. only the no. 1 strip is folded to make the corner). Pin onto the batting/wadding only. Pin along the 45 degree fold to form a neat edge *(fig. 25)*.

FIG. 25

There is no need to cut off the excess from the bottom (no. 2) fabric strip along the fold, unless a very light fabric is used and the seam is visible. In this case, leave a 2.5 cm (1 in) seam along the folded 45 degree edge and cut off the excess fabric. Do the same for the opposite corner. Pin along the raw edge of the fabric, smoothing out the creases with your free hand. Pin at right angles to the edge, along all four sides of the quilt and only onto the batting/wadding.

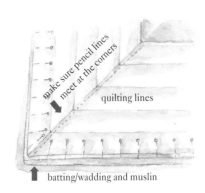

FIG. 26

11. The muslin at the back of the quilt is mitred at the corners as for the top fabric of the quilt. Unpin the muslin and fold a 45 degree corner on the muslin as in step 10 above. Turn the quilt over for easier handling. It is not necessary to cut off any excess fabric along the no. 2 strip of the muslin. Tack with cream or white thread along the muslin fold and remove the pins. Turn quilt right side up again.

12. Quilt through all the layers of fabric along the 45 degree fold *(fig. 26)*. Use two strands of matching thread or top stitch by machine. Sew through all three layers and remove the pins along the mitred corners only. Do not remove the pins along the raw edge of the fabric at this stage, or cut off excess batting/wadding or muslin.

FIG. 27

Quilt the fabric strips

1. Tack the layers of fabric, batting/wadding and muslin together so that the fabric does not move. Use an inexpensive machine thread and an embroidery needle for tacking.

2. Working from the edge of the fabric blocks outwards, tack so that the horizontal lines and the vertical lines are four fingers apart *(fig. 27)*. Tack along the centre of the drawn quilting lines. Do not tack on the drawn lines as the tacking threads will then be sewn down with the quilting stitches, making them difficult to remove.

Remember to tack along the raw edges of the sides of the quilt too, tacking all three layers together. Remove all the pins.

3. Use two strands of matching embroidery thread and tiny running stitches or quilting stitches to quilt by hand, along the drawn pencil line through all the layers. You may wish to machine stitch instead, using a matching thread. It is important that you have a large table to hold the quilt so that there is no pull on the fabric while you quilt or sew.

4. Do not cut off the excess batting/wadding and muslin at this stage.

HINT

❖ *You may like to take the quilt to a reputable curtaining shop that quilts commercially. They use industrial sewing machines to quilt along the drawn lines much faster than by hand.*

Sewing on the backing

1. Turn the quilt to the wrong (muslin) side and pin on the sheet or backing, from the centre outwards to the edges.

2. Tack in place as you did for the fabric sides of the quilt, leaving the edges of the sheet or backing longer than the quilt. (Do not cut the edges at this stage.)

3. Turn the quilt to the right side and pin along the raw edge of the fabric, with the pins at right angles to the edge, 3-5 cm (1-2 in) between each pin. Pin through all the layers *(fig. 28)*. (*See Preparing the block for a cushion or quilt*, page 35 – the quilt is prepared in exactly the same way.) Zig-zag along the raw edge of the fabric through all four layers. Remove pins.

4. Cut off excess batting/wadding, muslin, sheet or backing along the zig-zag line.

HINT
Keep the cut-offs to fill cushion pads.

Sewing on the lace or cord

❖ Decide if you'd like to sew lace or cushion cord into the grooves created by joining the blocks, and along the edges of the quilt for a balanced look.

❖ Cord or lace is sewn on by hand and definitely enhances the quilt but it is quite acceptable to leave the quilt free of lace or cord if you prefer.

If you have chosen the cord finish, *see Finishing a cushion with cord*, page 39 (the cord is sewn onto the quilt in the same way as for the cushion). Carefully cut the stitches where the cord starts and ends at the top and bottom seams of the blocks (in the same way as you did for the cushions). Stitch the raw ends of the cord tails, as for the cushion, and insert the tails in the quilt, leaving 5 cm (2 in) hanging over the sides of the quilt. These tails will also be stitched to prevent unravelling. *See fig. 29* for how to sew on the lace and cord. Leave the edges of the quilt and mitred corners free of cord or lace – this will be sewn on once the quilt has been attached.

If you have chosen a lace finish, pin and sew the lace on as for the cord, but stitch by hand along the two edges of the lace to anchor it to the quilt. Use running stitch or back stitch in a matching thread, or use blind hem stitch (*see Stitch the binding to the back of the cushion, fig. 11b* (page 42), for blind hem stitch). The stitches are only sewn through the lace, fabric and a section of the batting/wadding. It is not necessary to sew through all of the layers.

It is also not necessary to oversew the raw edges of lace as for the cord – the lace will be folded, wrong sides together, at the starting and ending points to make a hem. The lace that

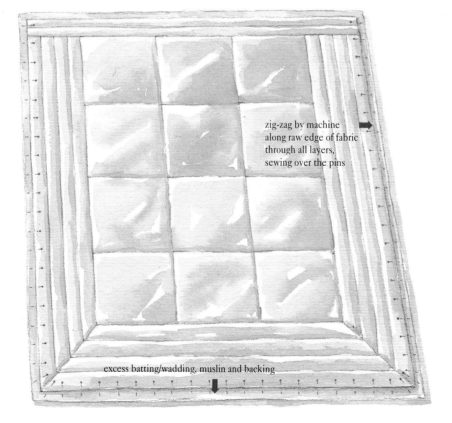

zig-zag by machine along raw edge of fabric through all layers, sewing over the pins

excess batting/wadding, muslin and backing

FIG. 28

ROUNDING THE CORNERS OF A QUILT LOOKS ATTRACTIVE AND ALLOWS THE QUILT TO HANG NEATLY TO THE FLOOR

hangs over the sides of the quilt will be stitched down when the binding is joined to the quilt.

Rounding the corners

❖ Before finishing the quilt, you may like to round the two bottom corners of the quilt. Rounding the corners looks attractive and allows the quilt to hang neatly to the floor.

❖ See quilt diagram (*fig. 14* on page 45) and note the rounded corners. Draw the desired curve lightly in pencil, as follows:

1. Make a paper pattern for a rounded corner. Measure from the top of the mattress edge to the floor *(fig. 30)*. Cut a piece of string to this length. Tie the string to a pencil and staple or pin the other end of the string to the corner of the paper. Draw the curve onto the paper and cut along the drawn line of the pattern *(fig. 31)*.

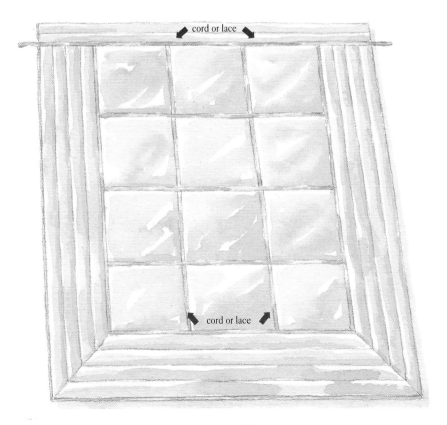

cord or lace

cord or lace

FIG. 29

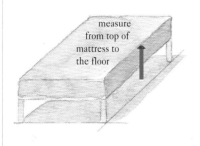
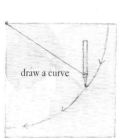
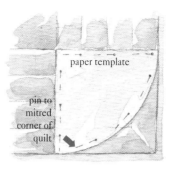
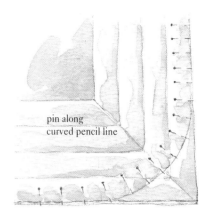

FIGS. 30, 31, 32 AND 33

2. Take the curved pattern and pin it to the mitred corner of the quilt *(fig. 32)*. Use a 2B or HB pencil to draw the curve onto the quilt.

3. Pin along the curved pencil line. Place pins 2.5 cm (1 in) apart, pinning at right angles to the edge *(fig. 33)*. Pin into the batting/wadding as you did for *Sew the backing slips on* (*see* page 36).

❖ Zig-zag along the pinned line, sewing over the pins. Stitch through all the layers. Remove the pins.

❖ Cut off the excess fabric, batting/wadding, muslin and sheeting or backing along the zig-zagged edge of the curve.

Finishing with binding

Before deciding how wide the binding strips need to be, place the quilt on the bed. Measure how much longer the quilt must be to hang to the floor or above the night frill. The measurements below will give a 6 cm (2¹/4 in) wide binding. If you need wider binding, use the extra 3 m (3¹/4 yds) purchased (*see How much fabric do I need?*, page 44). Calculate the width of the folded binding (i.e. the size once sewn onto the quilt, for example 13 cm (5 in)) as follows: 13 cm (5 in) (or required width) x 2 + 4 cm (2 in) for the folds = 30 cm (12 in) strips are cut.

1. MAKING THE BINDING

There is no need to cut the fabric strips on the cross of the cloth (bias) to make the binding for the quilt. In fact, the fabric puckers less if cut along the length of the fabric.

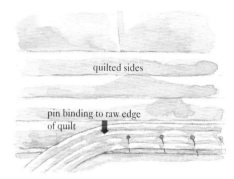

quilted sides

pin binding to raw edge of quilt

FIG. 36

❖ Use the remaining 3 m (3¹/4 yds) strips to make the binding (*see How much fabric do I need?*, page 44, and *fig. 13*, page 45 – the darker areas show the 3 m (3¹/4 yds) strips that remain after cutting strips for the sides).

FOR A 6 CM (2¹/4 IN) WIDE BINDING:

❖ Cut four strips 16 cm (6 in) wide x 3 m (3¹/4 yds) long.

❖ Join three of the strips to make a 9 m (9³/4 yd) strip – keep the fourth strip for the top of the quilt.

MAKE THE BINDING AS FOLLOWS:

a. Use a fabric starch and an iron.

b. Spray starch onto the wrong side of the fabric, fold the two raw edges, wrong sides together; press *(fig. 34)*.

fold 2 cm (1 in) and press

wrong side of fabric

16 cm (6 in)

fold 2 cm (1 in) and press

FIG. 34

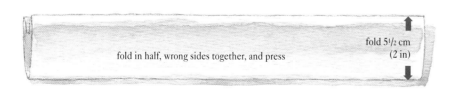

fold in half, wrong sides together, and press

fold 5¹/2 cm (2 in)

FIG. 35

c. Fold the two folded edges with the wrong sides together again and press *(fig. 35)*.

2. SEWING ON THE BINDING

a. With right sides together, pin the binding so that the raw edge of the binding lies on top of the zig-zagged edge of the quilt *(fig. 36)*.

b. Place the pins at right angles to the edge, starting at the top of the right or left hand side of the quilt and ending at the opposite edge. Do not pin the binding to the top part of the quilt at this stage.

c. As you round the corners, pin folds into the binding fabric to create a smooth, round corner. Pin until you reach the top of the left- or right-hand side of the quilt.

d. Machine stitch along the first pressed fold in the binding, i.e. the fold nearest to the edge of the quilt. Sew through all five layers, sewing over the pins if preferred, or removing them as you sew.

e. Remove all the pins.

f. Open the stitched-on binding strips so that the wrong side is lying on the work surface (i.e. the right side is showing). Pin the top binding (i.e. the binding on the top part of the quilt) as before, stitching from the one raw edge to the other raw edge of the binding through all the layers *(fig. 37)*.

g. Remove all the pins.

3. FILLING BINDING WITH BATTING/ WADDING STRIPS AND SEW

❖ To make the binding look like a bubble or thick roll, the binding is filled with batting/wadding strips before being sewn onto the backing of the quilt. This is optional, however. To fill the binding with the batting/ wadding strips, turn the quilt to the wrong side so that the backing shows.

a. Cut thin batting/wadding into strips 12 cm (5 in) wide and as long as possible. (Use the batting/wadding left over from the sides of the quilt i.e. 3 m (3¹/4 yds) long).

b. Fold the binding over to the back of the quilt. Fold the batting/ wadding strips in half and insert the batting/wadding in between the binding as you fold. Allow the folded section of the batting/wadding to lie against the folded part of the binding to form a neat, rounded edge. Fill the binding with batting/wadding as you fold and pin along all four sides of the quilt *(fig. 38)*.

c. Once the binding is folded and neatly pinned to the back of the quilt, it can be hem stitched in place using a matching thread. *(See fig. 11b*, page 42, *Stitch the binding to the back of the cushion* for hem stitch.)

HINTS

❖ *Join the batting/wadding strips with loose whip stitches so that all of the binding is filled with batting/wadding.*

❖ *Do not sew the binding on by machine – this will result in the stitching showing on the right side of the quilt.*

❖ *Do not pull the stitches too tight as this will cause the binding to pucker.*

pin top binding from raw edge of stitched binding to opposite raw edge

binding

edge of quilt

stitched binding opened flat

FIG. 37

backing of quilt

insert folded batting/wadding between folded binding and pin in place

folded binding

FIG. 38

OTHER PROJECTS

In this chapter, both the beginner and the advanced needleworker will be able to create these personalised gifts and original, eye-catching pieces for the home. The projects are attractive, fun and easy to make. Unlike the other projects, the Wedding Gifts are not embroidered through the batting/wadding and muslin.

A FRAMED GALLERY

These framed pictures are made using the *Still Life* and *Shelley* designs.

Materials

❖ *See Material requirements*, page 9.

– 15 cm (6 in) strip of iron-on Vilene or fusible webbing;

– two or three different shades of pink or peach polysilk, taffeta or glazed cotton for flower shapes and the fabric vase in the *Still Life* design;

– green or blue polysilk, taffeta or glazed cotton for the fabric leaves;

– 50 x 50 cm (20 x 20 in) square very thin batting/wadding;

– 50 x 50 cm (20 x 20 in) square poly-silk, taffeta or glazed cotton for the background block;

– 50 x 50 cm (20 x 20 in) square muslin for backing the batting/wadding;

– six-strand skeins embroidery thread: one green and three different shades of pink or peach;

– silk ribbon: about 4 m (4¼ yds) each of green and two different shades of pink or peach;

– beads (optional) in a matching or complementary colour for the centre of the flowers; and

– usual sewing aids, including a 35.5 cm (14 in) quilting hoop.

Method

1. Trace the shapes in *figs. 1 and 2*, according to your chosen design, onto the shiny side of the Vilene.
2. Follow the instructions under *Combining candlewicking with fabric shapes*, page 29.
3. *See Framing the block*, page 33.

TEA COSY

The *Bianca* design was used here. The size of the tea cosy pattern is standard but may be lengthened or widened accordingly. Trace the design onto tracing paper. Make one normal and one reversed copy and join.

FIG. 1 SHELLEY PATTERN

FIG. 2 STILL LIFE PATTERN

Materials

❖ *See Material requirements*, page 9.

– 2 x 50 cm (20 in) squares of fabric for front and back of tea cosy;

– 2 x 50 cm (20 in) squares of fabric in complementary shade for lining;

– 2 x 50 cm (20 in) squares of batting/wadding;

– 2 x 50 cm (20 in) squares of muslin for backing the batting/wadding;

– six-strand skeins of embroidery thread: one the same colour as the background, one green and two shades of pink or chosen colour for the roses;

– beads (optional) in a matching colour for the centre of the roses;

– 1 m (1 yd) bias binding to complement the colour of the cosy; and

– usual sewing aids, including a 35.5 cm (14 in) quilting hoop.

Method

Only the front of the tea cosy is embroidered in this design. If you wish to embroider both sides, follow the steps below, but make two embroidered sides and join the wrong sides together, then sew on the bias binding.

1. Take one of the 50 cm (20 in) squares of fabric for the front of the tea cosy and press to remove creases.

2. Follow the instructions on page 26 and embroider the tea cosy design.

3. Pin the tea cosy fabric onto the batting/wadding and zig-zag around the drawn outline of the cosy through all three layers. (*See Preparing the block for a cushion or a quilt*, page 35.) Cut off the excess batting/wadding, muslin and fabric *(fig 3)*.

4. Using the quilted tea cosy side as a guide, draw the shape for the back of the cosy onto the remaining fabric square. Place the background fabric square onto the remaining batting/wadding and muslin squares. Pin the layers together and zig-zag along the drawn line through all layers. Cut off

FIG. 3

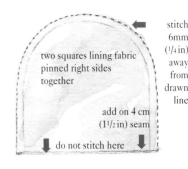

FIG. 5

FIG. 4

FIG. 6

excess fabric, batting/wadding and muslin. There are now two sides for the tea cosy, exactly the same size *(fig. 4)*.

5. Take the two squares of lining fabric and pin, right sides together. Draw the cosy outline onto the wrong side, using the embroidered cosy as a guide. Do not remove the pins. Add a 4 cm (1½ in) seam to the bottom edge.

6. Place the foot of the machine on the edge of the drawn line so that a 6 mm (¼ in) seam is added, and stitch the lining squares together. Stitch from one side along the curved edge to the other side, leaving the bottom of the cosy open. Cut the lining shape 6 mm (¼ in) away from the sewn line *(fig. 5)*.

7. Pin the two tea cosy sides together, wrong sides facing, with the pins at right angles to the edge. Sew through all six layers from side to side, leaving the bottom edge open. Leave a 6 mm (¼ in) seam. Remove the pins *(fig. 6)*.

8. The bias binding will be pinned along the sides and top curve of the cosy before you insert the lining. To make the bias binding you will need a 1 m (1 yd) length cut across the grain of the fabric. The strip will be 4 cm (1½ in) wide. Press a 6 mm (¼ in) seam along the two raw edges so that the wrong sides are facing. Fold in half again and press in place *(fig. 7)*.

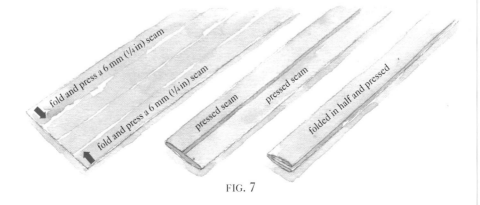

FIG. 7

9. Take the bias binding, open it up and with the right sides facing, pin it to the tea cosy so that two raw edges meet, pins at right angles to the edge. Sew through all seven layers along the first pressed fold in the bias binding. Remove the pins *(fig. 8)*.

pin bias binding to cosy

FIG. 8

10. Fold the binding over to the back of the tea cosy, allowing the pressed fold of the binding to fold in as you take it to the back of the tea cosy. Pin the binding in place on the tea cosy fabric *(fig. 9)*.

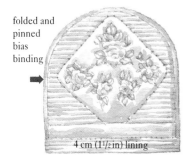

folded and pinned bias binding

4 cm (1¹/₂ in) lining

FIG. 9

lining folded and pinned

FIG. 10

11. Take the lining shape but do not turn it right side out. Insert it in the cosy like a glove (fold in half to find the centre point). The bottom edge of the lining should protrude by approximately 4 cm (1¹/₂ in). Turn this edge over, wrong sides together, so that the raw edge of the lining reaches the zigzagged edge of the cosy. Turn over again to make a neat hem lying on the tea cosy. Pin in place *(fig. 10)*.

12. Use a matching thread and blind hem stitch, stitch the binding to the back of the cosy and the lining hem to the bottom of the tea cosy at the front and back.

HINTS

❖ *When pinning the background fabric to the pattern and tracing the design onto the fabric, remember to add on the extra seams at the bottom and sides of the cosy where indicated on the design. It is important to trace the curved outline and bottom straight line of the pattern onto the fabric as this makes cutting easier when completing the cosy. Draw the tea cosy and outline of the design onto the centre of the fabric square and only cut to size once the cosy has been embroidered. Remove the fabric from the hoop and smooth out the creases.*

❖ *It is important to add an extra 4 cm (1¹/₂ in) seam to the bottom of the tea cosy shape* (fig. 3). *This 4 cm (1¹/₂ in) seam will be folded over to the right side of the tea cosy to make a neat hem along the bottom edge.*

TRAY CLOTH OR PLACE MAT

This project was made using the *Rose Garland* design and combines fabric shapes with candlewicking. Make a beautiful set of place mats or perhaps a tray cloth to match the *Tea Cosy* (page 55).

If you only want to use embroidery stitches instead of incorporating fabric shapes, ignore the materials marked with an asterisk (❖).

Materials (to make one cloth)
See Material requirements, page 9.

– 50 x 50 cm (20 x 20 in) square fabric for the front;

– 50 x 50 cm (20 x 20 in) backing ;

– 50 x 50 cm (20 x 20 in) square very thin batting/wadding;

– 50 x 50 cm (20 x 20 in) square muslin to back the batting/wadding;

❖ a strip green fabric for the leaves;

❖ a strip of pink or peach fabric for the rose;

❖ 10 cm (4 in) strip of iron-on Vilene or fusible webbing;

– six-strand skeins of embroidery thread – one green, one pink or peach and one the same shade as the background for quilting;

– beads (optional) for the centre of the roses;

– usual sewing aids, including a 35.5 cm (14 in) hoop;

– pattern, traced or copied from the book; and

– 1.8 m (1³/₄ yds) of bias binding in a complementary shade.

Method 1

USE ONLY EMBROIDERY STITCHES TO MAKE UP THE DESIGN

1. Follow the instructions on pages 23-33, *Candlewicking and quilting step-by-step.*

2. Take the 50 cm (20 in) square of fabric for the front; draw a 48 x 37 cm (19 x 14¹/₂ in) rectangle onto this.

3. Trace the design onto one end of the rectangle.

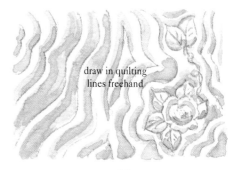

draw in quilting lines freehand

FIG. 11

4. Draw in the quilting lines free-hand *(fig. 11)*. These lines will be quilted through all the layers.

5. Place the fabric, batting/wadding and muslin layers into the 35.5 cm (14 in) hoop and embroider as in step 1, page 58.

6. Once the embroidery and quilting is complete, remove from the hoop.

Method 2

USE CANDLEWICKING AND FABRIC SHAPES TO MAKE UP THE DESIGN

We have used fabric for the rose and leaf shapes and candlewicked the raw edges on the background fabric. The shapes are simple, easy to make and save having to fill the shapes with embroidery stitches.

1. Follow the instructions on page 29, *Combining candlewicking with fabric shapes*.

2. Take the 50 cm (20 in) square of fabric for the front and draw a 48 x 37 cm (19 x 14$\frac{1}{2}$ in) rectangle on it.

3. Draw the shapes in *fig. 12* onto the shiny side of the Vilene or fusible webbing.

4. Glue on the fabric shapes using a soft glue stick, trace the remaining detail onto the fabric and draw in the quilting lines freehand *(fig. 11)*.

5. Candlewick and quilt as shown on page 32, *Candlewicking and quilting the design*. If using beads, sew them on at the centre of the roses. Remove the fabric from the hoop and finish quilting the areas that were covered by the

hoop by hand. (It is not necessary to move the hoop in sections. The corners can be quilted without a hoop if you prefer.)

6. Do not cut off the excess batting/wadding and muslin at this stage.

Completing the tray cloth or place mat

The tray cloth or place mat is not turned inside out at any stage of the finishing process. The backing is joined, wrong sides together, and bias binding is attached along the raw edges of the layers, following the steps below:

1. With wrong sides together, place the embroidered and quilted block on top of the backing fabric.

FIG. 12 ROSE GARLAND PATTERN

2. The cloth or mat must face right side up when pinning. Pin on the embroidered block through all the layers, pinning at right angles to the edge. Allow the batting/wadding, muslin and backing to overlap the edge of the embroidered cloth or mat. This excess will be cut off later, once you have zig-zagged along the raw edge of the embroidered cloth or mat.

3. Leaving a 3 mm (1/8 in) seam, zig-zag through all four layers along the edges of the embroidered fabric. Zig-zag along the drawn rectangle. Cut off the excess fabric, batting/wadding, muslin and backing close to the zig-zagged stitches.

4. Apply the bias binding as shown for the *Tea Cosy*, page 57. Hem stitch binding in place on the backing side.

HINT
Pre-wash and press backing fabric if it is cotton or a cotton blend.

CHRISTENING BIB AND ROBE

A christening is always an important event in the family and a candle-wicked bib or robe is an ideal present for the baby.

CHRISTENING BIB

I used the *Veronique* design and fabric shapes for the roses and leaves. You may prefer to only embroider the design, in which case you should ignore the materials marked with an asterisk (❖).

Materials
❖ *See Material requirements*, page 9.

– 30 x 30 cm (12 x 12 in) square polysilk or cotton fabric for the front;

– 30 x 30 cm (12 x 12 in) square very thin batting/wadding;

– 30 x 30 cm (12 x 12 in) square muslin for the backing;

– 30 x 30 cm (12 x 12 in) square fabric for lining the bib;

❖ a piece of green or blue fabric for the leaves;

❖ a piece of peach or pink fabric for the roses;

❖ 10 x 10 cm (4 x 4 in) square piece of iron-on Vilene or fusible webbing

– six-strand skeins of embroidery thread: one green, one peach or pink;

– beads (optional) for the centre of the roses;

– 1.5 m (1³/4 yds) bias binding in a complementary shade;

– usual sewing aids, including a 10 in (25 cm) hoop; and

– pattern, copied or traced from the book.

Method
1. Follow instructions on page 29 (*Combining candlewicking with fabric shapes*). Draw the shapes in *fig. 13* onto the shiny side of the Vilene and cut out each shape 3-4 mm (1/8 in) away from the pencil line. Iron these shapes onto the wrong side of the chosen colour fabric for the roses and leaves. Cut out each shape along the drawn pencil line. Place each fabric shape on a glass table with a light underneath it, or against a sunny window. Neatly trace all the detail on the Vilene onto the right side of the fabric. Set aside.

2. Using the 30 cm (12 in) square of fabric for the bib front, pin the pattern centrally onto the fabric with the wrong side of the fabric against the right side of the pattern. Draw the bib outline onto the right side of the fabric. Do not remove the pins at this stage.

3. First glue and press the fabric shapes onto the background using the pattern as a guide (first leaf, then rose shapes) onto the bib front. Draw in the remaining detail, i.e. the tear-drops, dots and buds that are not cov-

FIG. 13 VERONIQUE PATTERN

CANDLEWICKED PROJECTS CAN BE USED FOR INDOOR OR OUTDOOR LIVING

ered by the fabric shapes. Remove the pins and the pattern.

4. Insert the fabric, batting/wadding and muslin layers into the hoop as shown under *Candlewicking and quilting the design*, page 32. Candlewick and quilt as instructed in this chapter. Remove the fabric from the hoop.

5. With wrong sides together, place the embroidered front on top of the lining/backing square. Pin in place, pinning at right angles to the edge.

6. Leave a 3 mm (1/8 in) seam and zig-zag along the drawn outline through all the layers.

7. Cut off excess fabric close to the zig-zag stitch.

8. Apply the bias binding as shown in

add curved neck of binding, leaving enough on both sides to form the ties

FIG. 14

fig. 14, leaving lengths on both sides to form the ties. (Refer to page 57 on binding the *Tea Cosy* and how to make your own binding.)

9. Stitch the binding to the back of the bib. Stitch the binding together along the folded edge of the ties using a blind hem or whip stitch.

CHRISTENING ROBE

The Christening Robe, like the *Christening Bib* on page 60, is candlewicked using the *Veronique* design and uses the same embroidery stitches. I used an ordinary baby dress pattern and lengthened the skirt to 70 cm (28 in). Shorten or lengthen the skirt to suit your requirements.

Materials

Refer to the instructions on the dress pattern for how much fabric to purchase before following the method below. Also refer to *Material requirements*, page 9.

– 3-4 m ($3^1/4$-$4^1/2$ yds) of dress fabric depending on how wide you would like the skirt to be;

– 50 x 50 cm (20 x 20 in) square of background fabric for the front panel of the dress (this fabric must be the same as the dress fabric and will be embroidered);

– 50 x 50 cm (20 x 20 in) square very thin batting/wadding for backing the front panel fabric;

– 50 x 50 cm (20 x 20 in) square muslin to back the batting/wadding;

– 50 x 50 cm (20 x 20 in) square lining fabric to back the embroidered block once completed;

– buttons for cuff and neck (if required);

– six-strand skeins of embroidery thread: one green for leaves, one light and one dark peach, pink or blue for the flowers in the design;

– round pearl beads (optional);

– usual sewing aids, including a 35.5 cm (14 in) quilting hoop; and

– design traced or copied from the book.

trace design onto centre of panel

FIG. 15

fabric

batting/wadding

muslin

FIG. 16

Method

❖ Refer to *Candlewicking and quilting step-by-step*, page 23.

1. Use the dress pattern to draw the front panel onto the background fabric square.

2. Trace the design onto the centre of the panel *(fig. 15)*.

3. Place the panel, batting/wadding and muslin layers into a 35.5 cm (14 in) hoop as for the *Christening Bib* on page 60 *(fig. 16)*.

4. Embroider the detail of the design as described on page 26.

5. Remove the fabric from the hoop.

6. With wrong sides together, pin the lining square to the back of the embroidered block.

7. Tack the panel along the drawn line and cut off excess fabric, batting/wadding and muslin next to the stitched line.

cut, leaving required seam

FIG. 17

8. It is important to leave the seam width required on the actual pattern *(fig. 17)*.

9. Attach lace in a complementary colour along the hem, the sleeves and the neck of the robe, or as desired.

10. Sew on buttons (if necessary).

ROUND BASKET COVER

This basket cover, using the *Coral Reef* design, makes a superb birthday or Christmas gift. The basket used was 25 cm (10 in) in diameter and 15 cm (6 in) deep. Adjust the measurements if using a different size basket.

Materials

❖ Please refer to *Material requirements*, page 9.

– spray paint in any colour of your choice;

– round basket, 25 cm (10 in) in diameter, 15 cm (6 in) deep;

– 30 x 30 cm (12 x 12 in) square fabric for top of cover (polysilk or cotton);

– 30 x 30 cm (12 x 12 in) square batting/wadding;

– 30 x 30 cm (12 x 12 in) square muslin, to back the batting/wadding;

– 30 x 30 cm (12 x 12 in) square fabric for lining cover, in a darker shade;

– six-strand skeins of embroidery thread: one red, one navy, one green;

– beads, green or navy blue, for the centre of the flowers;

– 1.5 m ($1^1/2$ yds) bias binding in a complementary shade of green, red or navy blue;

– 40 cm (16 in) strip of fabric for handle and to make bows to decorate the basket;

– usual sewing aids, including a 25 cm (10 in) hoop;

– pattern traced from book; and

– quick-drying glue for attaching the fabric bows.

paper template

cut moon shapes at handles

FIG. 18

Method

1. Spray paint the basket inside and out according to manufacturer's instructions. Allow to dry.

2. Cut a paper template the same size as the opening of the basket. Fold the paper in half and draw a dotted line to indicate the position of the handles. Cut moon-shapes at the handles *(fig. 18)*.

3. Take the template and draw this shape onto the right side of the square fabric for the top of the cover. Draw the two moon shapes for the handles.

4. Pin the pattern in the centre of the circle and trace the design onto the fabric. Take care to draw a neat and accurate outer circle.

5. Place the fabric square onto the batting/wadding and muslin. Place these layers into the hoop as instructed on page 27. Candlewick and quilt as shown on page 32. If using beads, sew them onto the centre of the flowers. Remove the fabric from the hoop.

6. With wrong sides together, place the embroidered top on top of the lining/backing square.

7. Pin in place, pinning at right angles to the drawn circle edge.

8. Leave a 3 mm (¹/₈ in) seam and zig-zag along the drawn line through all four layers. Cut off excess fabric, close to the zig-zag stitch.

9. Apply bias binding as shown in *figs. 19* and *20* below, leaving a 10 cm (4 in) tail on either end to tie the cover onto the basket handle. (Refer

A ROUND BASKET COVER (CORAL REEF PATTERN) MAKES A SUPERB GIFT

to *Binding the tea cosy*, page 57, for how to make your own binding.) The width of the binding for this cover is 5 cm (2 in) wide and 1.5 m (1¹/₂ yds) long, cut across the grain.

10. The binding forms the ties for the cover. Stitch it to the back of the cover

and continue stitching along the ties, sewing the folded edges together with a blind hem or whip stitch.

11. Decorate the basket by winding fabric around the handle. Make stiff fabric bows and glue them onto the side. If you are making the basket as a Christmas gift, glue small fruit or berry shapes to the sides.

HINTS

❖ *Take the design with you when purchasing a basket to ensure a good fit. If you cannot find a basket to fit this design, why not enlarge or reduce the pattern on a photocopier to make it fit?*

bind the moon shapes first

FIG. 19

leave 10 cm (4 in) tails

FIG. 20

ADD A PERSONAL TOUCH TO BOUGHT LINEN BY EMBROIDERING THE MERMAN (LEFT) OR HIGH SEAS PATTERN (CENTRE)

❖ *If using a 25 cm (10 in) diameter basket, use the 25 cm (10 in) quilting hoop to draw the circle.*

❖ *Before delivering the gift, place a bottle of champagne or home-made bread inside the basket. If you are making a basket for a baby's nursery, cover it with pastel-coloured fabric and fill it with with baby products.*

EASY WEDDING GIFTS

Embroidering the design

Most of us have very busy schedules, yet a wedding warrants a more personal gift. Why not purchase a ready-made tablecloth, guest towel or set of serviettes and add a personal touch with an embroidered design?

Choose a tablecloth or guest towel with a beautiful finish but little or no detail on the fabric itself. Embroider the corners of the cloth or serviettes,

and along one edge of the towel. These Wedding Gifts will not be embroidered through the batting/wadding and muslin.

There are six small designs to choose from: *High Seas, Camouflage, Merman, Orient, Rosebud* or *Pebble*.

Materials

– purchased tablecloth, guest towel or serviettes;

– six-strand skeins embroidery thread: two or three different shades (one green for leaves and two pink for flowers);

– usual sewing aids, including a 25 cm (10 in) or 35.5 cm (14 in) hoop;

– if necessary, strips of fabric to sew onto the edge of the cloth to make it big enough to fit into the hoop ;

– pattern traced from book; and

– tin of commercial spray starch.

Method

1. Trace the design onto the cloth as described on page 26.

2. If necessary, add on fabric strips so that the entire design fits in the hoop. *See fig. 6b*, page 26.

3. Pull the fabric taut in the hoop and candlewick the design as described on pages 27-29. Start and finish by running the tail ends of the thread under the adjoining stitches so that the back is neat and tidy, or separate the embroidery strands and tie knots, one on top of the other.

4. Remove the fabric from the hoop and remove any fabric strips. Wash in cold water to remove marks.

5. Hang up to dry.

6. Spray the wrong side of fabric with spray starch and iron until crisp. Fold your article neatly and it is ready to be wrapped!

S P R A Y M I S T

make 2 normal copies and 2 reversed copies

CRIMSON GLORY

make 2 normal copies and 2 reversed copies

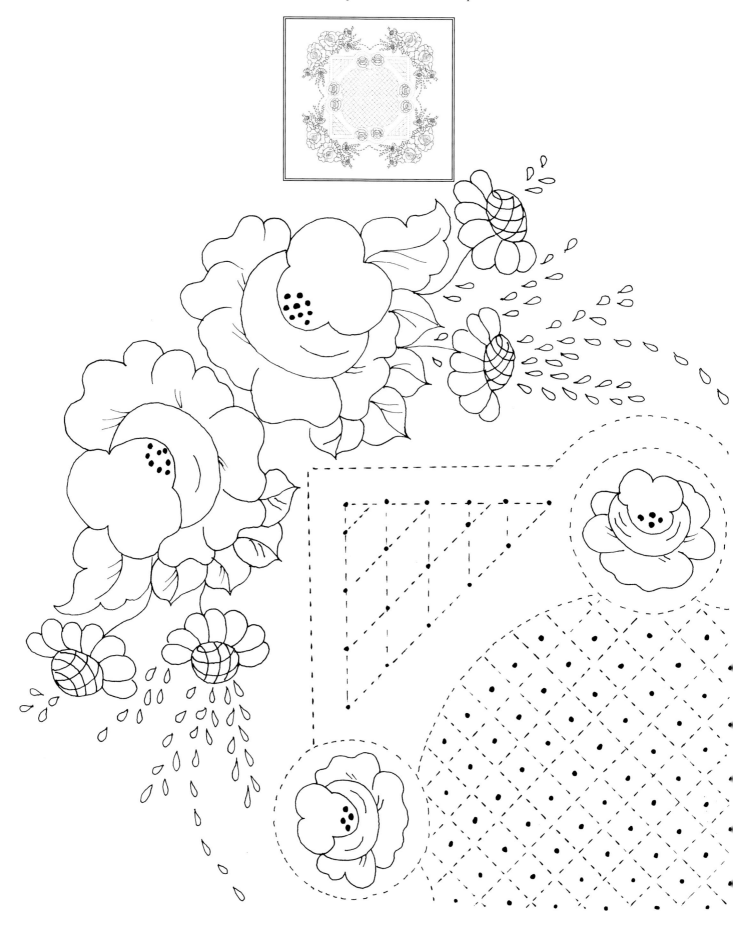

MONTE CARLO 1

make 1 normal copy and 1 reversed copy

M O N T E   C A R L O   2

make 1 normal copy and 1 reversed copy

CIRCLE OF ROSES
make 2 normal copies and 2 reversed copies

ALASKA

make 2 normal copies and 2 reversed copies

CLIMBING TALISMAN 1

make 1 normal copy and 1 reversed copy

CLIMBING TALISMAN 2

make 1 normal copy and 1 reversed copy

R A M B L I N G   R O S E

make 2 normal copies and 2 reversed copies

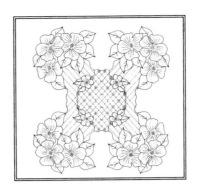

JAMELLE

make 2 normal copies and 2 reversed copies

PEACE ROSE

make 2 normal copies and 2 reversed copies

P A R A S O L 1

make 1 normal copy

PARASOL 2

make 1 normal copy

PARASOL 3

make 1 normal copy

PARASOL 4

make 1 normal copy

ENGLISH GARDEN 1

make 1 normal copy and 1 reversed copy

ENGLISH GARDEN 2

make 1 normal copy and 1 reversed copy

A M B I E N C E

make 2 normal copies and 2 reversed copies

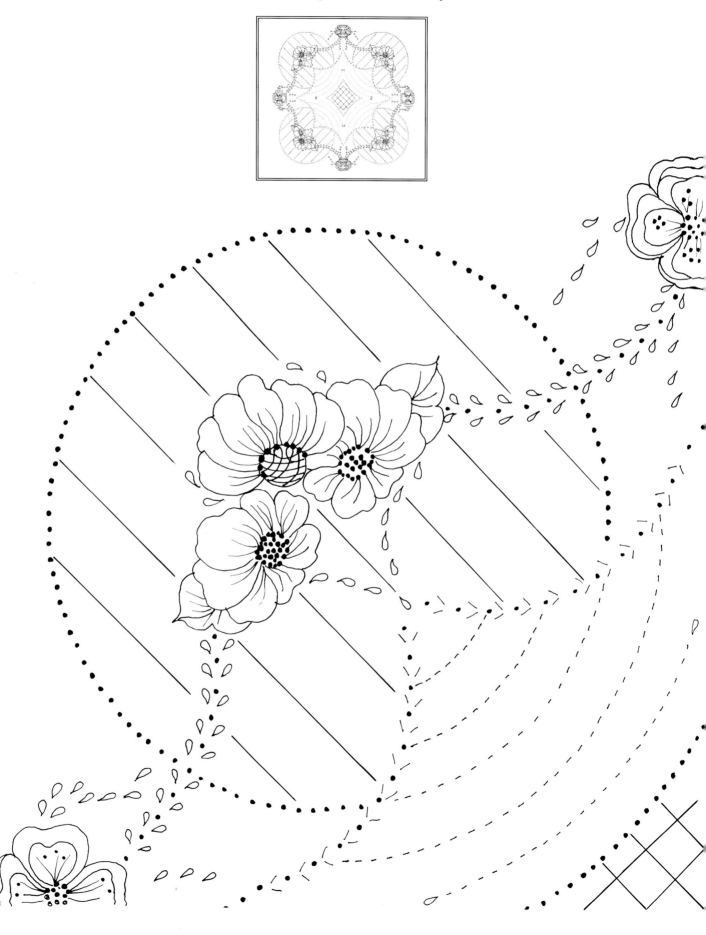

BALMORAL

make 2 normal copies and 2 reversed copies

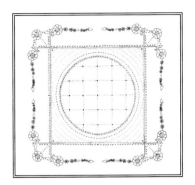

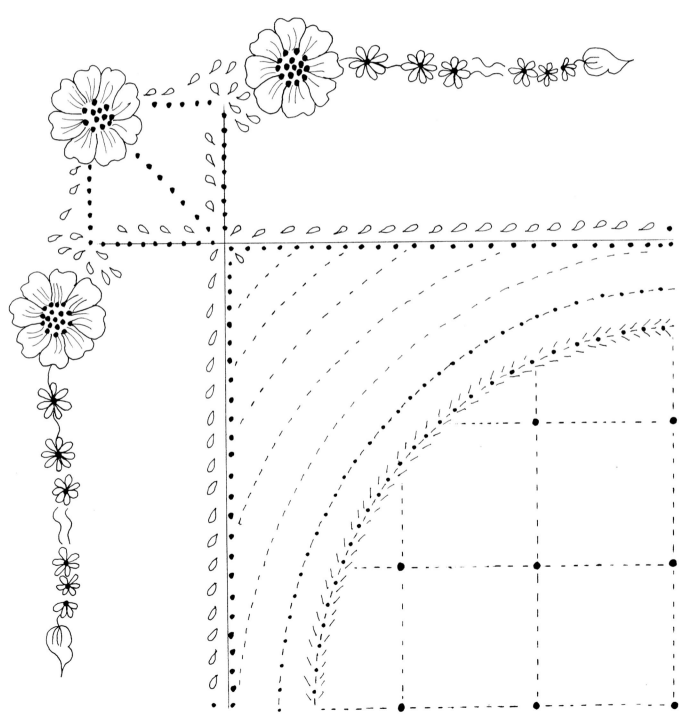

FANTASY

make 2 normal copies and 2 reversed copies

CONSTANTIA

make 2 normal copies and 2 reversed copies

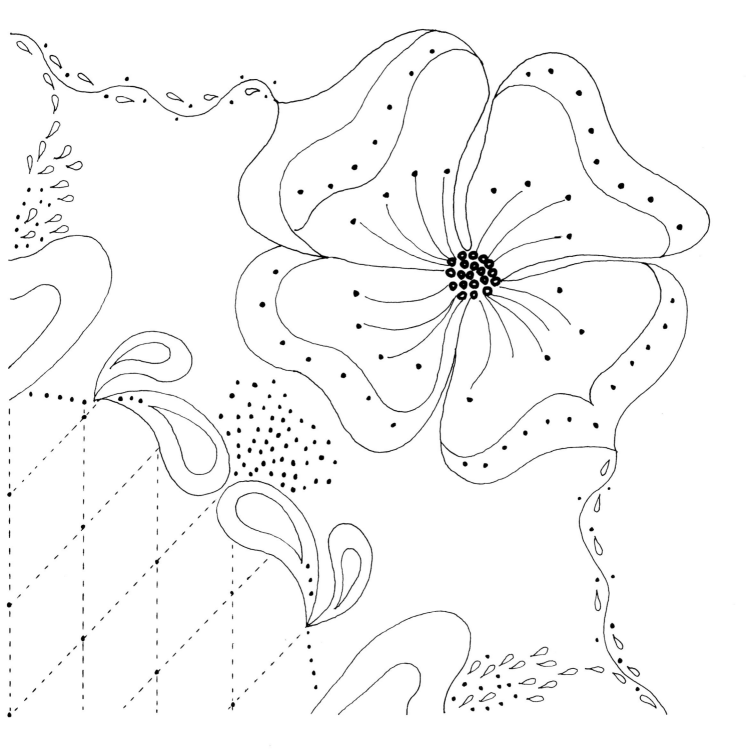

SERENADE

make 2 normal copies and 2 reversed copies

SARAH

make 2 normal copies and 2 reversed copies

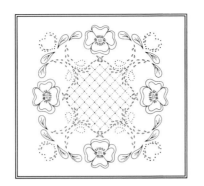

STILL LIFE

SHELLEY

BIANCA
make 1 normal copy and 1 reversed copy

Add a 1 cm (½ in) seam

Add a 2,5 cm (1 in) seam

ROSE GARLAND

CARNIVAL

VERONIQUE

CORAL REEF

HIGH SEAS

MERMAN

CAMOUFLAG.

PEBBLE

ROSEBUD

ORIENT